HOW DO WE KNOW
ANIMALS CAN THINK?

STEVE PARKER

RSVP ®

RAINTREE
STECK-VAUGHN
PUBLISHERS
The Steck-Vaughn Company

Austin, Texas

Published by Raintree Steck-Vaughn Publishers, an imprint of Steck-Vaughn Company

Commissioning Editor: Tom Keegan
Designer: Liz Black
Editors: Kate Scarborough, Maurice J. Sabean
Illustrators: Peter Bull, Aziz Khan. Linden Artists Ltd.: David Cook, Stewart Lafford, Ruth Lindsay, Jane Pickering, Clive Pritchard, David Webb. Bernard Thornton: Maurice Pledger, Fred Anderson, Robert Morton

Library of Congress Cataloging-in-Publication Data

Parker, Steve.
  Animals can think? / Steve Parker.
    p.   cm. — (How do we know)
  Includes index.
  ISBN 0–8114–3882–1
  1. Senses and sensation—Juvenile literature.   2. Cognition in animals—Juvenile literature.   [1. Animals.   2. Senses and sensation.]   I. Title.   II. Series.
  QP434.P368   1995
  591—dc20   94–19405
                                                              CIP
                                                              AC

Printed and bound in Hong Kong

1 2 3 4 5 6 7 8 9 0 HK 99 98 97 96 95 94

The words in boldface type are explained in the glossary.

Contents

HOW DO WE KNOW

What an Animal Is?

Animal or not?
The amoeba is a microscopic blob of jelly that lives in a pond. Its whole body is a single **cell**. It cannot be an animal, since animal bodies have many cells.

It is in a group called protists.

Can animals think? People who get to know animals by looking after them, feeding them, and training them would probably say, "Yes!" People who consider thinking whether a dog could play chess or a cat could multiply 6 by 9 might say, "No!" The answer depends partly on what we mean by animals and also on what we mean by think. So first—what is an animal?

The answer may seem easy. Animals move, eat food, and breathe using lungs or **gills**. Well, not necessarily. Some animals, such as sponges and barnacles, do not move. Some animals, such as mayflies, have no mouths and cannot eat. Some animals, such as flatworms, have no lungs or gills. On these pages you will learn about a range of animals, how their bodies vary, and how they live very different lives.

A dolphin lives in water but has lungs, so it must surface to breathe air.

THE RANGE OF ANIMALS

There are two main groups of animals. One is the invertebrates, such as worms, insects, spiders, crabs, and starfish. They do not have backbones. The other group is the vertebrates, or backboned animals, which include fish, **amphibians, reptiles**, birds, and **mammals**.

Butterfly (insect)

Worm

Spider

Jellyfish

Leopard (mammal)

Fish

Crocodile (reptile)

Frog (amphibian)

Eating
Animals need food to live and grow (see pages 18–19). Some feed all through life, like birds. Others, like some insects, feed during only one part, or stage, of life.

Moving

Most animals move (see pages 12–13). They use legs, wings, and tails, wiggle their bodies, squirt water, or use other methods. They move to find food and shelter, and to avoid danger and enemies. A bird can fly huge distances in one day in search of food.

A snake's tongue can "taste" the air as it flicks in and out.

A chipmunk eats a nut, but it watches and listens for danger.

Sensing

Animals use their senses to detect features of the world around them. The main senses are seeing, hearing, smelling, tasting, and touching (see pages 20–29). Some animals have extra senses, such as detecting electricity or magnetism (see pages 30–31).

Plants that eat

Animals are not the only living things that eat food. Plants such as the Venus's-flytrap and the sundew live in poor, thin soil. Their roots take in little nourishment. So the plants get extra nutrients by trapping flies and other small creatures, dissolving them, and absorbing the juices.

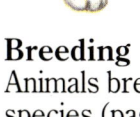

Breeding

Animals breed to produce more of their own species (pages 34–35). A female and male of the same species mate, and after some time, babies are born. Some babies hatch from eggs outside the female, as with birds and insects. Others develop inside the female and are born live, as with mammals and some reptiles.

What Thinking Is?

To think about something, you consider it in your mind. You assess the situation, consider the actions you might take, choose one, and do it. If a fast car approaches, you think fast and simply—jump out of the way! To solve a riddle, you think in a slower, more complicated way. Your thoughts produce your behavior. Animals, like humans, respond to different situations with their behavior. So they must have ways of assessing what to do and choosing an action to take. Their ways of "thinking" are extremely simple and automatic compared to ours. But they carry out different behavior in different situations, as these examples show.

Unthinking?
When a dog sees and smells food, its mouth waters. Around 1900, scientist Ivan Pavlov rang a bell each time he fed a dog. Soon the dog's mouth watered on hearing the bell, even when there was no food present. This "unthinking" action is called a conditioned reflex.

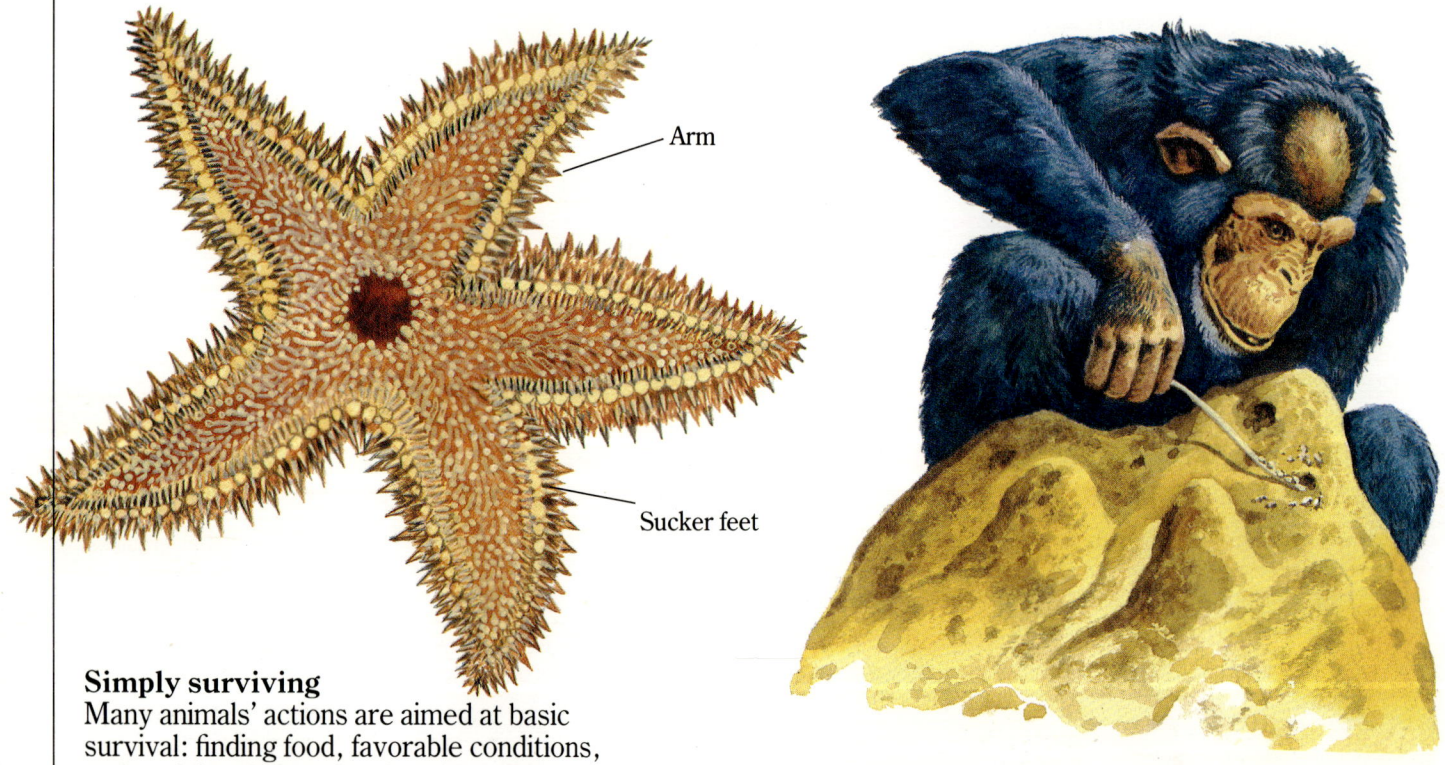

Arm

Sucker feet

Simply surviving
Many animals' actions are aimed at basic survival: finding food, favorable conditions, and avoiding dangerous situations. The starfish is a simple animal with a simple set of reactions, such as crawling, pulling open a shellfish to eat, hiding under a stone, and curling up if attacked. Yet even with such simple behavior and seemingly little thought, millions of starfish survive.

Making tools
The animals most similar to humans are apes, chimps, and gorillas. They can plan ahead and think about how to solve a problem by making and using tools. A chimp can pick up a small twig, strip off the leaves, and poke it into a termites' nest. The termites crawl onto the twig, and the chimp pulls the twig out and eats the termites.

Storing food

Many animals prepare for the future by storing food in times of plenty to be eaten later, when food is short. Mice store seeds in their burrows. Squirrels bury nuts. The bird called the shrike hunts small animals, such as insects, frogs, and lizards. It pushes some of them onto sharp thorns or barbed wire and returns to eat them later. This behavior has earned the shrike the nickname of "butcher-bird."

Being trained

Animals such as dogs and horses have been bred so that they can be trained and used by people. The animal realizes that if it learns the commands and obeys them, it will be rewarded.

Using tools

A few animals make tools, like the chimp (opposite). But many animals use tools. The Pacific sea otter uses a stone as a hammer. It dives to the seabed and gathers shellfish and a stone then returns to the surface. The otter puts the shell on its chest and smashes it with the stone to break it open and get at the tasty flesh inside.

TELLING OTHERS

Honeybees visit flowers for their sugary **nectar**, which is food for hive members. If a bee finds flowers with nectar, it goes back to the hive and does a figure-eight "dance" on the upright honeycomb. The movements of the dance show the direction of the nectar-laden flowers relative to the sun. Other hive members can then find the flowers and bring back the nectar.

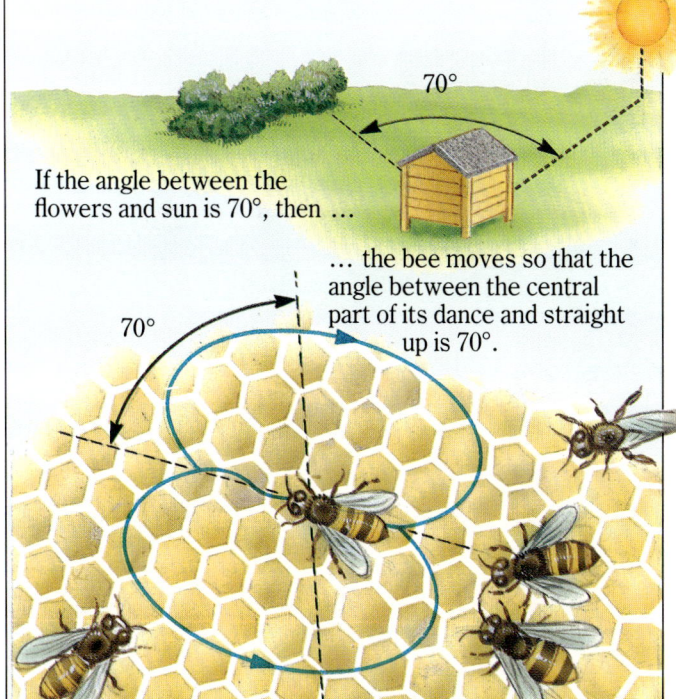

If the angle between the flowers and sun is 70°, then …

… the bee moves so that the angle between the central part of its dance and straight up is 70°.

70°

70°

Taking advantage

Many types of animals have learned to live around houses and other buildings, and take advantage of the shelters we build. The North American raccoon can set up home in the corner of an outbuilding, or in the roof space of a house. These places are similar to its natural den under a tree, log, or rock.

Where Thinking Takes Place?

NERVOUS SYSTEMS

A nervous system is made up of nerves. Each nerve is a bundle of microscopic nerve cells (shown on the right). The nerves form a branching network throughout the body.

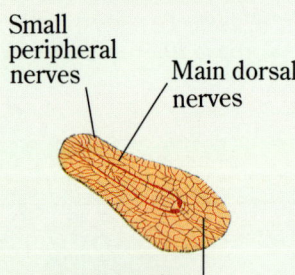

Small peripheral nerves

Main dorsal nerves

Cerebral ganglion (simple "brain")

Flatworm
This small creature has a simple nervous system, with only a few nerves. The nerves come together at the front end to form a simple "brain."

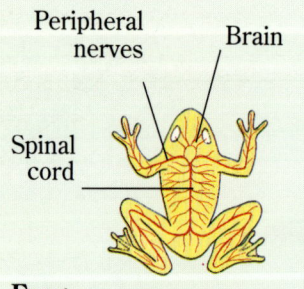

Peripheral nerves

Brain

Spinal cord

Frog
The frog has a complicated nervous system, consisting of a brain, a main nerve called the spinal cord, and **peripheral** nerves spreading throughout the body.

Through the ages, people have cut animals open to see what is inside and experimented on animals to find out what their body parts do. This may sound cruel. But the resulting knowledge enables us to understand how living things work. This biological information tell us that thinking takes place in an animal's brain, which is part of its **nervous system**. The nervous system consists of microscopic parts known as nerve cells. These carry tiny pulses of electricity, called nerve signals, throughout the body. The signals convey information about what the animal is sensing, thinking, and doing.

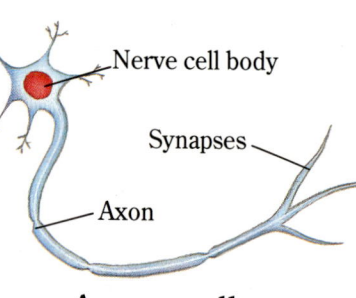

Nerve cell body

Synapses

Axon

A nerve cell
This type of cell has a long, thin part called an axon, like an electrical wire. Junction points, known as synapses, pass nerve signals to other nerve cells.

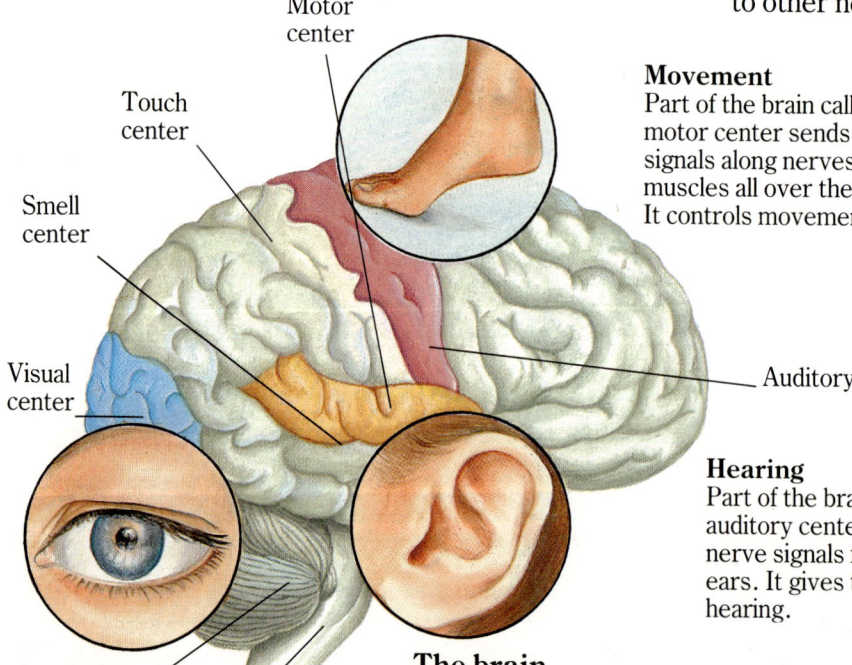

Motor center

Touch center

Smell center

Visual center

Auditory center

Cerebellum

Spinal cord

Movement
Part of the brain called the motor center sends nerve signals along nerves to muscles all over the body. It controls movements.

Hearing
Part of the brain called the auditory center receives nerve signals from the ears. It gives the sense of hearing.

Seeing
Part of the brain called the visual center receives nerve signals from the eyes. It gives the sense of sight (vision).

The brain
Experiments and the results of natural injuries show that the brain is the control center for all body processes. It is a bulging network of millions of nerve cells, connected to other body parts by hundreds of nerves. Different areas of the brain are specialized to do different jobs (as shown throughout this book). Some areas receive nerve signals from the sense **organs**, such as the eyes and ears. Other areas send out nerve signals to the muscles, telling them when to move.

BRAIN POWER

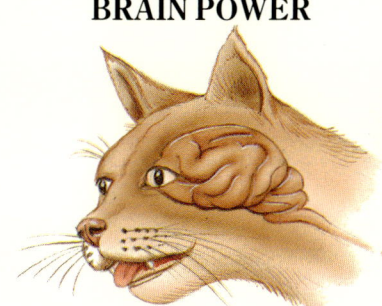

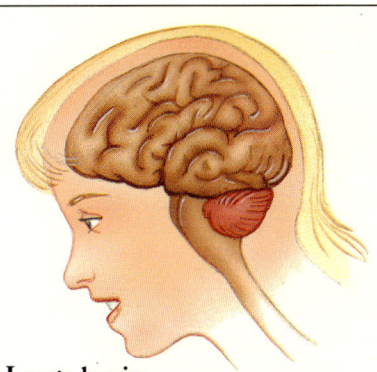

Small brain
Studies show that the bigger an animal's brain is relative to the size of its body, the more "intelligent" or "clever" that animal is. A snake has a small brain compared to its body size. It has a very limited ability to learn. Most of its actions are for basic survival.

Medium brain
In proportion to body size, a cat's brain is bigger than a snake's brain. A cat can learn new actions and adapt its behavior to new situations. The areas of the brain dealing with balance, sight, and hearing are larger than those in the snake's brain.

Large brain
In the whole animal kingdom, the animal with the largest brain relative to its body size is the human. The brain makes up 1/50th of the total body weight, compared to 1/100th in a dolphin, 1/700th in an elephant, and 1/1,200th in a cow.

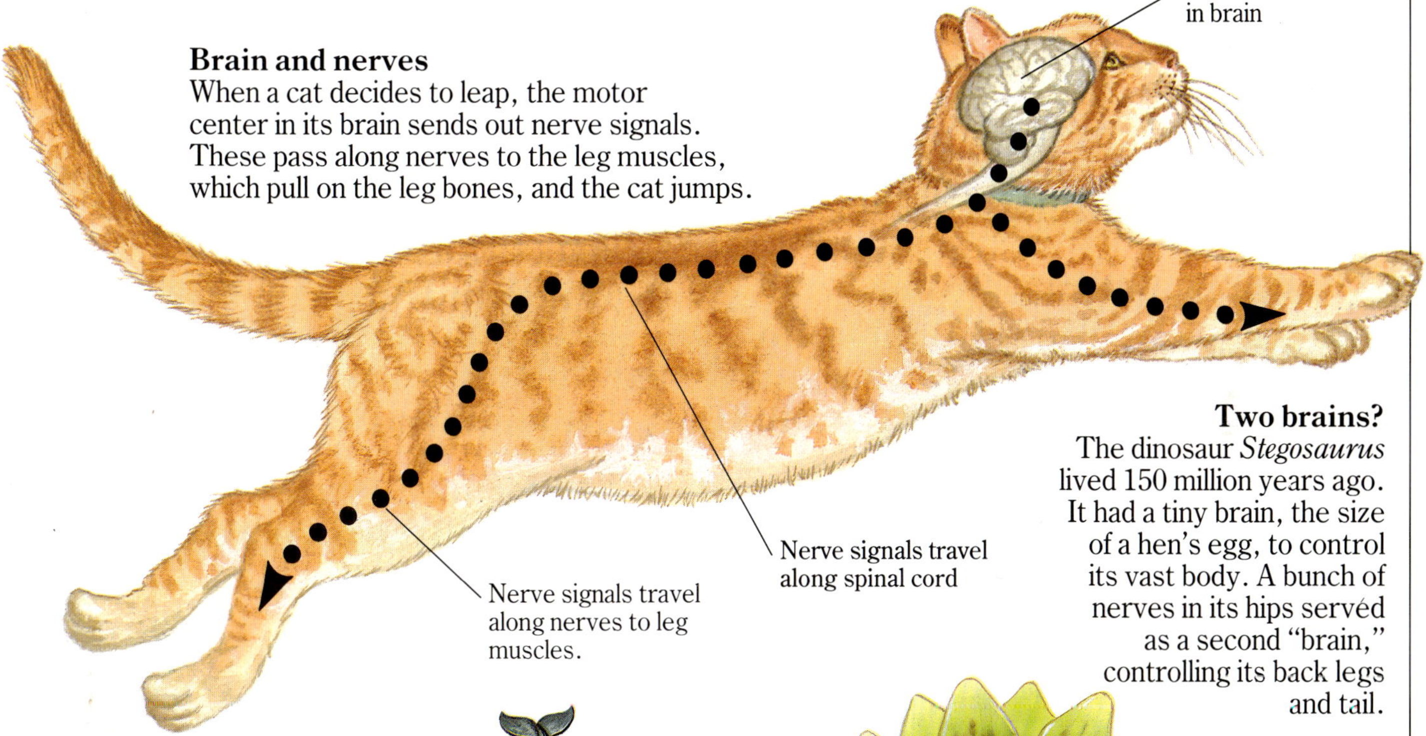

Brain and nerves
When a cat decides to leap, the motor center in its brain sends out nerve signals. These pass along nerves to the leg muscles, which pull on the leg bones, and the cat jumps.

Motor center in brain

Nerve signals travel along spinal cord

Nerve signals travel along nerves to leg muscles.

Two brains?
The dinosaur *Stegosaurus* lived 150 million years ago. It had a tiny brain, the size of a hen's egg, to control its vast body. A bunch of nerves in its hips served as a second "brain," controlling its back legs and tail.

Nerve junction in hips

The sperm whale's brain is about the size of a small TV.

The biggest brain
The animal with the largest brain is the sperm whale. It weighs 17.5 pounds (8 kg), compared to a human brain at 3 pounds (1.4 kg). But the whale has a huge body. Its brain is only 1/5,000th of its body weight.

Brain

Fish Can Breathe?

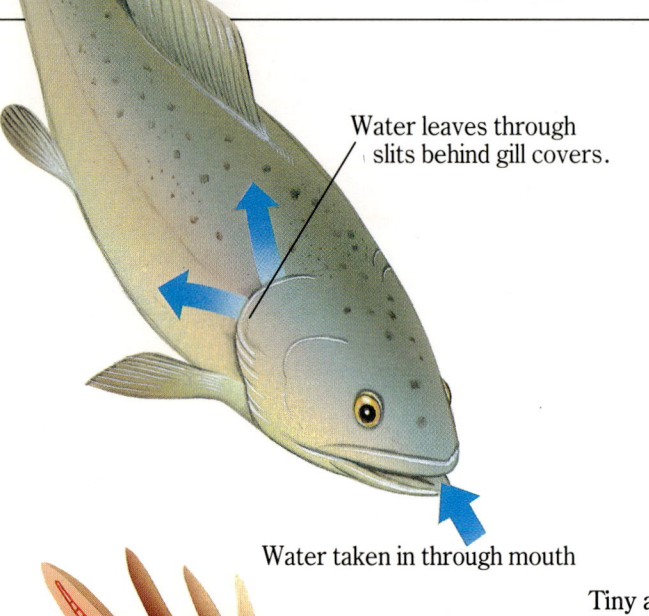

Water leaves through slits behind gill covers.

Water taken in through mouth

W e know that fish breathe, because like all animals, they need **oxygen**. Oxygen is a vital ingredient in the **chemical** processes inside the body that break down food to give the **energy** necessary for life (see pages 18–19). If an animal cannot get regular supplies of oxygen, it suffocates and dies. Land animals get their oxygen from the air around them, since oxygen makes up one-fifth of the air. Water animals, such as fish, use gills to take in oxygen dissolved in the water. The parts of the body specialized for breathing and obtaining oxygen make up the respiratory system.

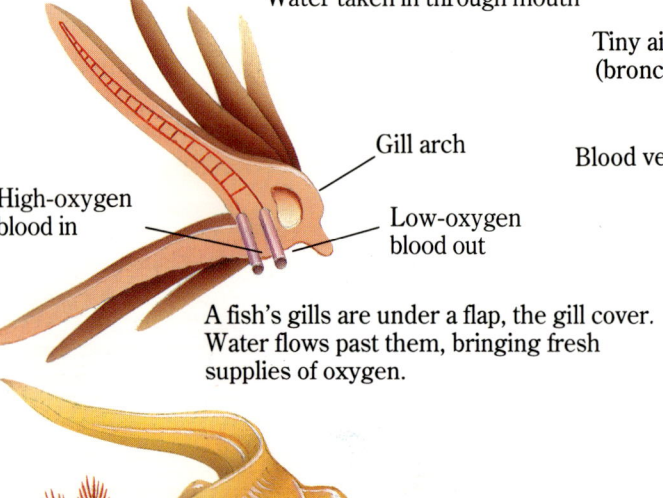

High-oxygen blood in

Gill arch

Low-oxygen blood out

A fish's gills are under a flap, the gill cover. Water flows past them, bringing fresh supplies of oxygen.

A salamander's feathery gills stick out into the water.

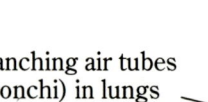

Tiny air tube (bronchiole)

Blood vessels

Alveolus

Air in and out through nose and mouth

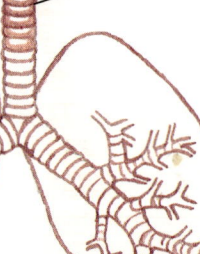

Windpipe

Branching air tubes (bronchi) in lungs

Spongy lung made up of millions of alveoli

Breathing with gills
Most water creatures have gills for breathing. These are feathery parts, usually just behind the head. They have a plentiful **blood supply**. Oxygen from the water seeps through the thin covering of the gills, into the blood inside. The blood flows throughout the body, carrying the oxygen to all body parts.

Breathing with lungs
Some land creatures breathe using lungs, two spongy organs in the chest. They contain air tubes that branch and get smaller, ending in millions of tiny air sacs, called alveoli, which contain microscopic blood vessels. When a breath is taken, air passes down the windpipe into the alveoli. Oxygen passes from the air into the blood flowing through the vessels, which carries it throughout the body.

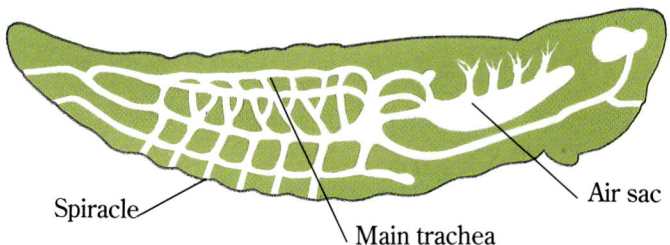

Spiracle
Main trachea
Air sac

Breathing with trachea

Small animals, such as insects, have a network of air tubes, called trachea, inside the body. These lead to openings at the skin's surface, called spiracles, which allow oxygen-containing air into the body. As the insect moves, the air tubes bend and squeeze. This pushes out stale air and sucks in fresh air.

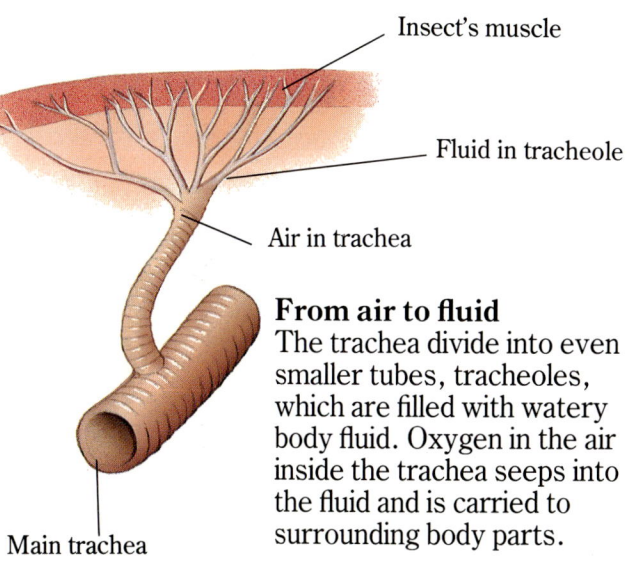

Insect's muscle

Fluid in tracheole

Air in trachea

From air to fluid

The trachea divide into even smaller tubes, tracheoles, which are filled with watery body fluid. Oxygen in the air inside the trachea seeps into the fluid and is carried to surrounding body parts.

Main trachea

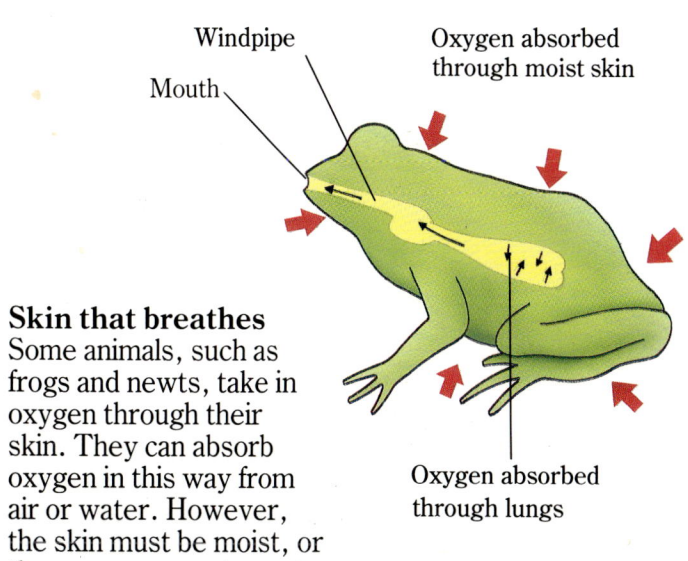

Windpipe
Mouth
Oxygen absorbed through moist skin
Oxygen absorbed through lungs

Skin that breathes

Some animals, such as frogs and newts, take in oxygen through their skin. They can absorb oxygen in this way from air or water. However, the skin must be moist, or the oxygen cannot pass through. If a frog gets too dry, it may suffocate!

BREATHING AIR UNDERWATER

Whales

Several types of mammals, which breathe air, live in the ocean. They hold their breath for long periods, as they swim after their food underwater, then return to the surface to breathe fresh air. Tracking by radio and **sonar** shows that the sperm whale holds its breath for almost two hours and swims more than 1.2 miles (2 km) below the water's surface.

Seals

Seals and sea lions hunt underwater for their food of fish, squid, shrimp, and similar creatures. The Weddell seal is the champion seal diver. It can go underwater more than 1,900 feet (600 m) and stay under for more than an hour.

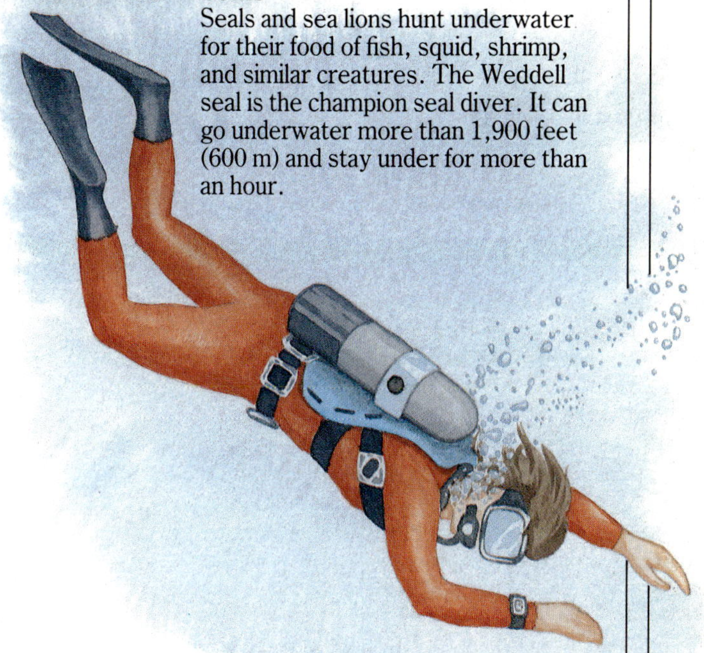

Humans

Most humans cannot hold their breath for more than a minute, especially when underwater. For longer dives, people take scuba tanks containing a special mixture of gases to breathe. They can descend to depths of about 400 feet (130 m).

How Animals Move?

W e know that sea anemones can move because people have watched them! The sea anemone is a simple animal, consisting of a stalk-shaped body topped by a crown of stinging tentacles. It may seem to sit still on the same rock forever. But the anemone can move very slowly, in a shuffling fashion, to find a better position on a nearby rock.

All animals can move, and they use muscles to do so. In most creatures, the movement is obvious, as in a galloping horse. Some animals, such as sea lilies, mussels, and barnacles, move only at a certain stage in their lives, often when they are very small. When adult, these aquatic (water-dwelling) animals do not have to move around in order to feed. Bits of food float to them in the seawater.

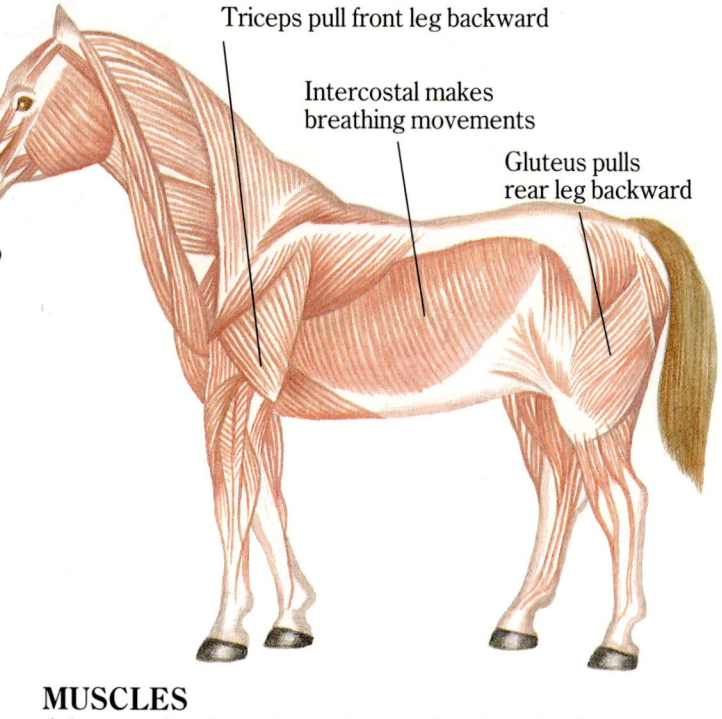

Triceps pull front leg backward

Intercostal makes breathing movements

Gluteus pulls rear leg backward

MUSCLES

A large animal, such as a horse, has hundreds of muscles. Each has a scientific name. Most muscles are attached to a bone at either end. As the muscle gets shorter, or contracts, it pulls on the bone and makes the animal move. Even tiny movements, such as an eye blink, are powered by muscles.

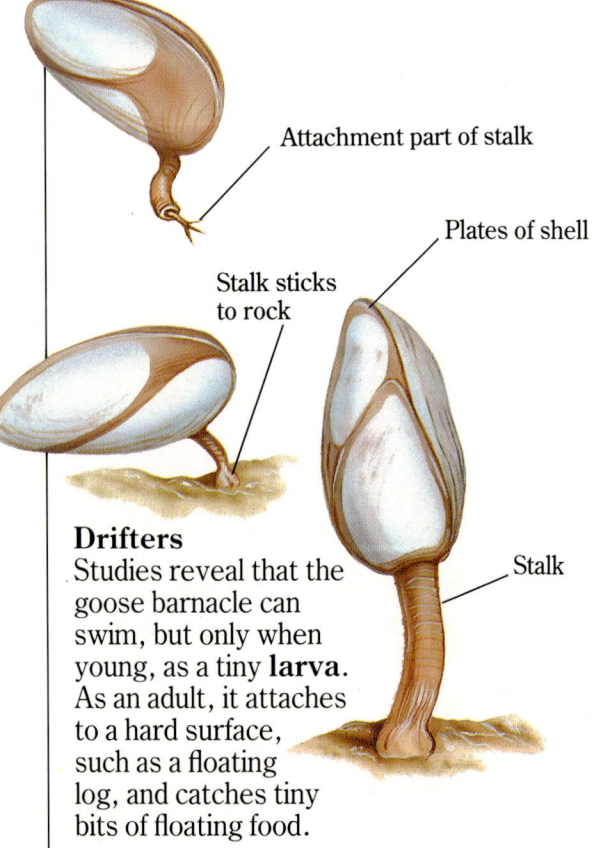

Attachment part of stalk

Plates of shell

Stalk sticks to rock

Stalk

Drifters

Studies reveal that the goose barnacle can swim, but only when young, as a tiny **larva**. As an adult, it attaches to a hard surface, such as a floating log, and catches tiny bits of floating food.

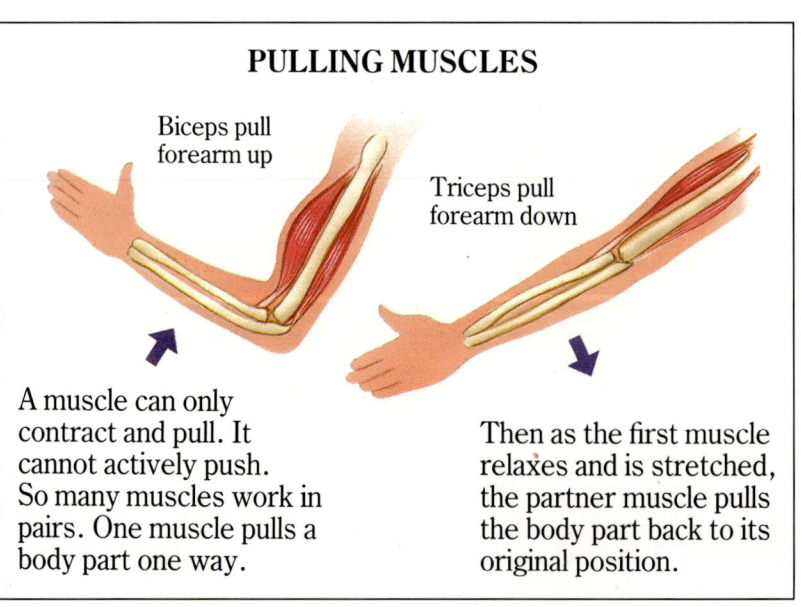

PULLING MUSCLES

Biceps pull forearm up

Triceps pull forearm down

A muscle can only contract and pull. It cannot actively push. So many muscles work in pairs. One muscle pulls a body part one way.

Then as the first muscle relaxes and is stretched, the partner muscle pulls the body part back to its original position.

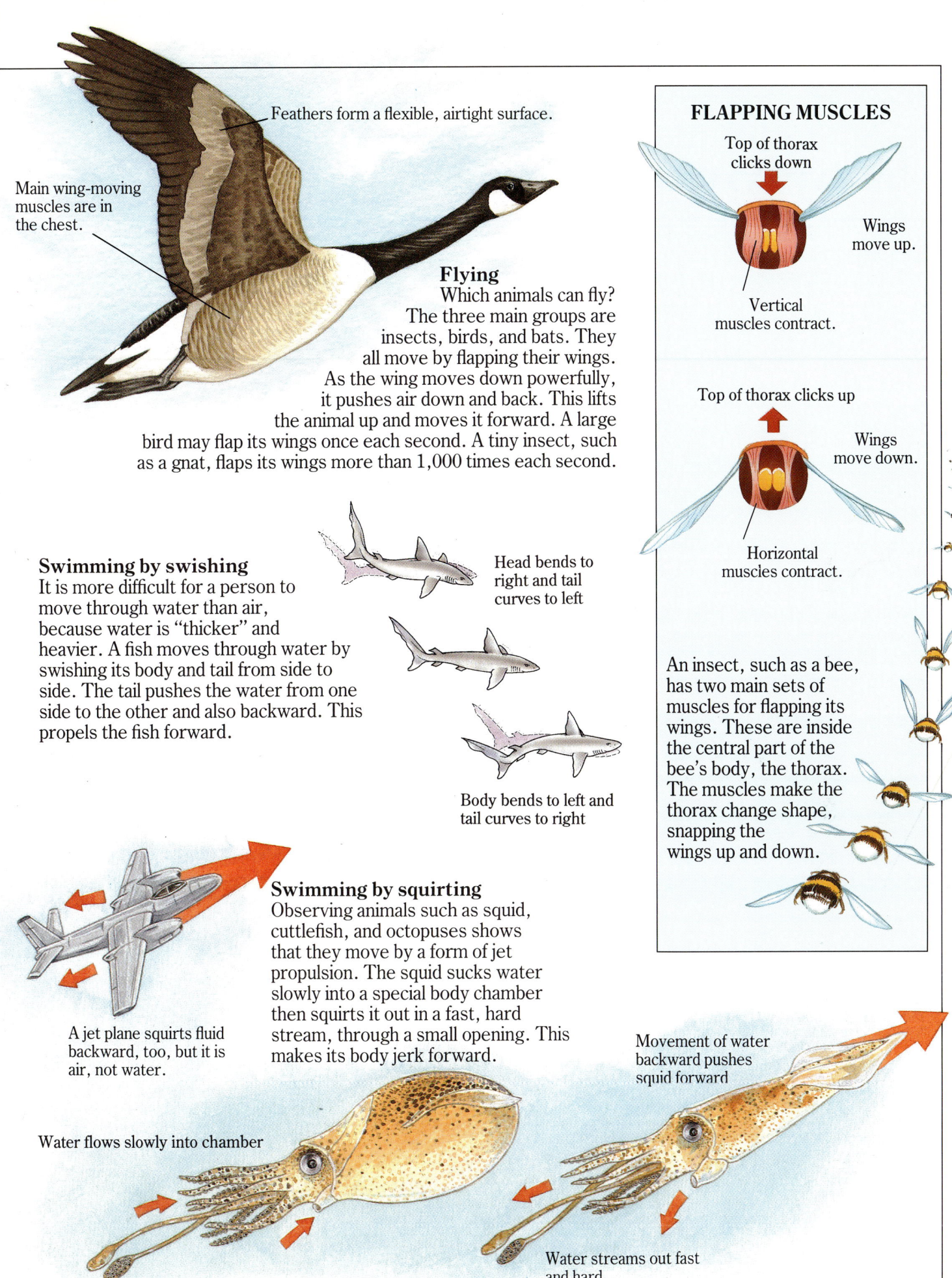

Feathers form a flexible, airtight surface.

Main wing-moving muscles are in the chest.

Flying

Which animals can fly? The three main groups are insects, birds, and bats. They all move by flapping their wings. As the wing moves down powerfully, it pushes air down and back. This lifts the animal up and moves it forward. A large bird may flap its wings once each second. A tiny insect, such as a gnat, flaps its wings more than 1,000 times each second.

FLAPPING MUSCLES

Top of thorax clicks down

Wings move up.

Vertical muscles contract.

Top of thorax clicks up

Wings move down.

Horizontal muscles contract.

An insect, such as a bee, has two main sets of muscles for flapping its wings. These are inside the central part of the bee's body, the thorax. The muscles make the thorax change shape, snapping the wings up and down.

Swimming by swishing

It is more difficult for a person to move through water than air, because water is "thicker" and heavier. A fish moves through water by swishing its body and tail from side to side. The tail pushes the water from one side to the other and also backward. This propels the fish forward.

Head bends to right and tail curves to left

Body bends to left and tail curves to right

A jet plane squirts fluid backward, too, but it is air, not water.

Swimming by squirting

Observing animals such as squid, cuttlefish, and octopuses shows that they move by a form of jet propulsion. The squid sucks water slowly into a special body chamber then squirts it out in a fast, hard stream, through a small opening. This makes its body jerk forward.

Movement of water backward pushes squid forward

Water flows slowly into chamber

Water streams out fast and hard.

Worms Know Where to Go?

If you carefully dig up an earthworm from the garden and leave it on the surface, it tries to burrow back into the soil again. The worm "knows" that it does not want to stay on the surface. It wants to get back underground. This is because worms are suited to, or adapted to, life in the soil. On the surface, their moist bodies would dry out, and they would die, or birds would catch and eat them.

Each type of creature is adapted to living in certain surroundings, like a pond, a forest, or a sandy seashore. A creature's surroundings are called its habitat. The creature tries to stay in its habitat, because it has the greatest chances of finding food and avoiding harm. Can you imagine a penguin living in a hot desert, or a camel in the ocean?

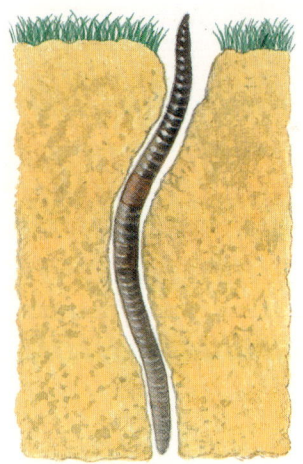

In the dark
A worm can detect the difference between light and dark. It moves away from the light and toward the dark, which usually means heading for damp, cool places under the ground.

Large forepaws and strong claws for tunneling

Below the ground
The mole is well adapted to its underground life. If brought to the surface, it detects the light with its tiny eyes, and immediately digs back into the soil.

In the jungle
The tiger lives in a jungle habitat, with dense undergrowth, trees, and tall grasses. Its stripes conceal the tiger as it stalks its prey. This way of merging with the background is called camouflage.

Camouflage
The striped pattern on the tiger's fur blends in with grass stems and branches.

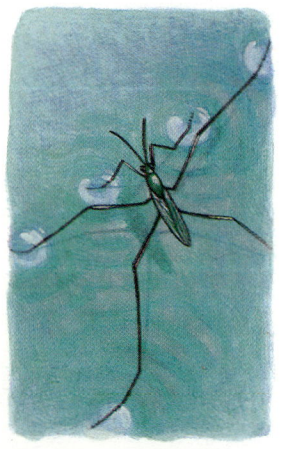

On the water
The pondskater flies, runs, and walks on water! This insect is very small and light. The tiny hairs on its feet do not break the surface tension, or "skin," on water, so the pondskater can slide across the surface.

In the air

The swift's long, powerful wings show that it spends almost all of its life in the air. It catches food in midair. It courts its partner and mates on the wing. It drinks by skimming over a pond or stream and dipping its beak into the water. It even rests and goes into a light sleep as it flies.

Nonslip feet

The sole of the polar bear's paw has a covering of stiff hair rather than the usual leathery skin. This gives a good grip on smooth ice.

Large feet for walking in snow and catching prey

On ice and snow

The polar bear's very thick, white fur suggests that it lives somewhere cold and white, where it can stay warm and camouflaged. Polar bears live in the snow and ice of the Arctic, in the far north near the North Pole. Under the thick fur and skin is a layer of fat, called blubber. Along with the fur, this helps to keep the bear's body heat in and the biting cold out.

HIGH AND LOW HABITATS

Wide hooves for firm grip

On the mountain

As with the tiger and polar bear, you can make a guess at the habitat of an animal from its body shape and features. The mountain goat has soft, wide hooves that provide a firm grip on the slippery, wet rocks found high in the mountains. Its legs are stocky and powerful, for climbing and leaping among the boulders. And its long fur keeps out the cold winds, rain, and snow.

In the desert

Deserts are very dry, and many are very hot during the day. Desert animals, like the desert skink, usually spend the day in burrows, away from the fierce heat of the sun. They come out in the cool of the night to look for food.

Scaly skin prevents moisture loss.

At the bottom of the ocean

In the dark depths of the ocean, many animals are black, like the gulper eel. This provides camouflage in the deep gloom. Food is scarce, so they have huge mouths to grab whatever they can. It may be weeks before another meal.

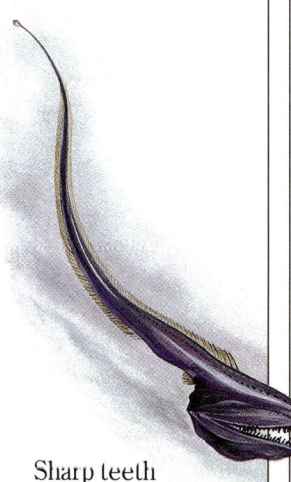

Sharp teeth prevent victim from escaping

Why Birds Build Nests?

To find out why birds build nests, you need to watch birds and the way they use their nests. To do this without disturbing the birds takes great skill and patience. Most birds use the nest for breeding. It is a relatively safe place to lay their eggs, and it becomes a home for the chicks when they hatch. Some birds use a nest outside the breeding season, as a place to shelter and rest.

Observations show that many other animals make nests, too, including insects and mammals. The nests are used for raising young, as shelters from bad weather, as resting places, and for escape and hiding. Some animals use ready-made holes, burrows, and caves for these purposes.

What's in a nest?

The building materials for a nest are usually taken from the surroundings. A bird in the grasslands uses grass stems and blades. A bird in a forest collects twigs, moss, and small leaves. The bird selects a fairly safe, sheltered place and weaves the parts together into a cup shape. Nests near towns and cities may have bits of wool, string, and paper in them.

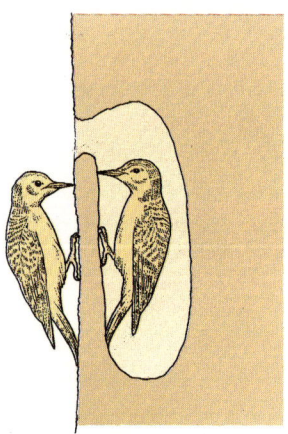

Nest holes and bowers

Birds such as woodpeckers (left) nest in holes inside tree trunks. They peck out the wood with their beaks and use the same hole for several years. The male bowerbird (right) makes a bower, or shelter, of sticks, leaves, feathers and other decorations, to impress the female before mating.

Weaving a nest

The male weaverbird constructs the breeding nest. He starts with a loop of vine, or creeper. Then he twines together creepers, stems, and strips of leaves, gradually building up a very intricate nest shaped like a hollow ball or flask. The nest hangs from a thin branch, so it is very difficult for predators, such as snakes or mongooses, to get inside and eat the eggs or chicks.

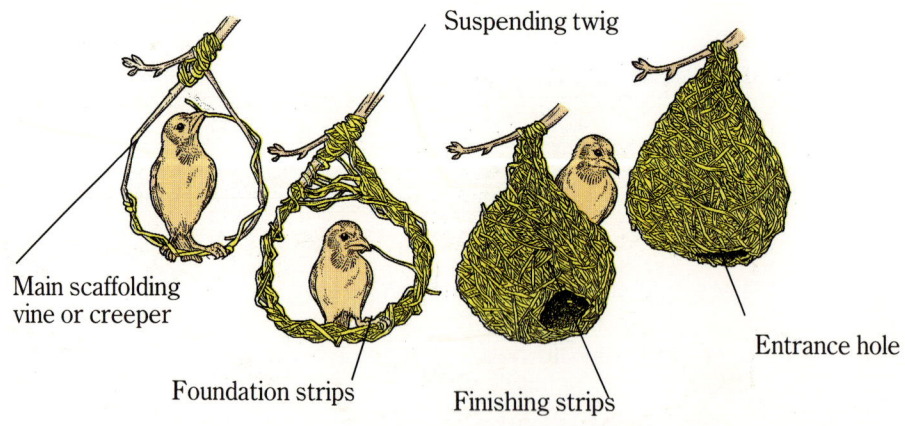

Suspending twig

Main scaffolding vine or creeper

Foundation strips

Finishing strips

Entrance hole

Fortress nest

Termites are small, defenseless insects, with soft bodies that would soon dry out in the hot sun. They can survive only by working together to build a huge nest from mud and earth. The mud dries to form a hard, protective mound, and the termites live in the cool, damp interior.

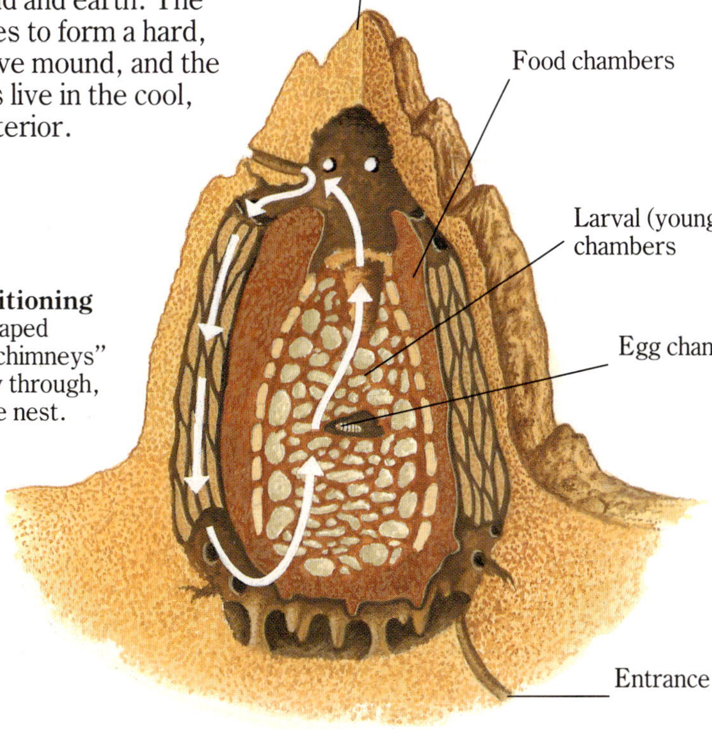

Air-conditioning
Funnel-shaped holes or "chimneys" let air flow through, cooling the nest.

Hard, baked walls

Food chambers

Larval (young) chambers

Egg chambers

Entrance hole

Platform nest

The gorillas of Africa spend most of their day on the ground, feeding on fruits, shoots, bark, stems, and leaves. At night baby gorillas and smaller females climb into trees and bend branches and twigs together to make a bowl-shaped sleeping platform. This helps to protect them from their main enemies, leopards. The adult males are big and strong, so they sleep on the ground.

Mid-lake nest

A beaver family builds a home base called a lodge, in the middle of a pool or lake. Part of the lodge is below the surface, with entrance tunnels from the surrounding water. Above surface level are dry platforms for feeding and resting, and a nest for the babies. The lodge walls are very strong, made from sticks, stones, and mud. The walls and the surrounding water are good protection against such enemies as wolves and lynxes.

Small hole for fresh air

Dam
The beavers may also build a dam to keep the lake's water level high throughout the year.

Sleeping chamber

Lodge wall

Underwater entrance

What Animals Like to Eat?

If you had a pet spider, you could offer it various foods to see which ones it preferred. This would give you some idea of whether or not spiders like to eat flies. But there are many kinds of spiders and many types of flies. The only sure way to find out what an animal eats is to watch it in nature.

Why do animals eat? Food provides energy for life processes and **nutrients** for bodily growth and maintenance. The food goes in through the mouth and passes through a long passageway called the digestive system. Here food is broken down, or **digested**, into very tiny pieces and absorbed into the blood, which carries the digested food to all parts of the body.

Feeding on fluids
A spider's web of sticky silk traps flies, moths, and other small creatures. Its poisonous bite kills the victim. The spider then sucks out its body juices, leaving the empty body shell and hard parts, like wings and legs.

Feeding on meat
Big cats, such as lions, tigers, and cheetahs, are hunters, or predators. They pursue their prey, leap on it, slash it with their sharp claws, and rip it with their long, pointed front teeth. Then they bite off and chew chunks of meat with their shearing back teeth. Animals that eat mainly meat and flesh are called carnivores. The main parts of the digestive system of such an animal are shown below.

Feeding on anything
Rats can eat and digest almost any kind of food, from insects and worms, chunks of meat, and gristle, to seeds, nuts, and leaves. Animals that eat plants and animals are called **omnivores**.

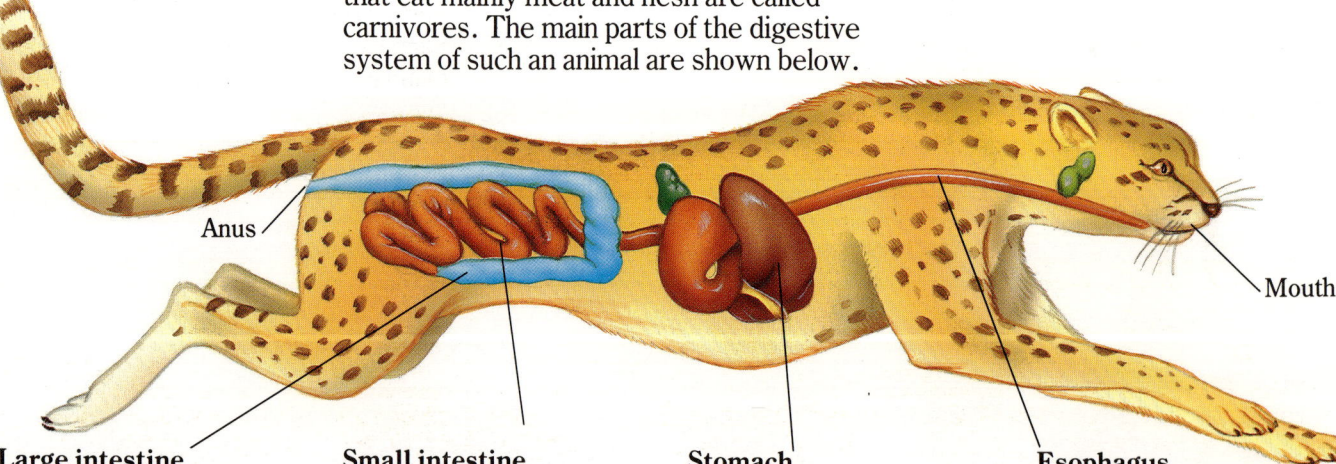

Anus

Mouth

Large intestine
This absorbs water and body salts from leftover, undigested food. It forms solid remains into droppings (feces), ready to leave the body.

Small intestine
Long and thin, the small intestine adds some more digestive chemicals to the food, making a sloppy soup. It absorbs the resulting nutrients into the body.

Stomach
This muscular bag stretches to hold the solid and liquid food. It squeezes and churns to pulp and squashes the food and adds strong digestive chemicals.

Esophagus
Swallowed food goes into this tube, which has strong muscles in its wall. The muscles squeeze the food along the esophagus into the stomach.

Feeding on insects

The anteater has no teeth. But it does have a long, sticky tongue. It pokes this into a nest of ants or termites. The small insects stick to the tongue, and the anteater licks them off and swallows them whole. Animals that eat small creatures such as insects are called insectivores.

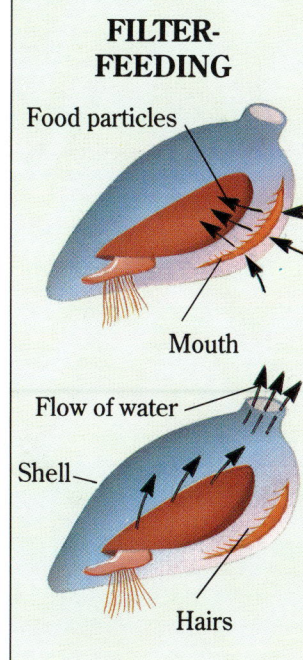

FILTER-FEEDING

Food particles

Mouth

Flow of water

Shell

Hairs

Shellfish cannot chase after their prey. They draw in seawater and filter out tiny bits of floating food. The food particles get caught in a net of tiny hairs and are slowly swept into the animal's mouth.

Feeding on fish

The anglerfish lies on the seabed. Its "fishing rod" is a spine on its back fin, with a fleshy "bait" at the end. Small fish come near to examine the bait, and the anglerfish gulps them into its huge mouth. Animals that eat fish are called piscivores.

Feeding on plants

Broad, flat-topped crushing teeth indicate a plant-eater, or herbivore. Some herbivores, such as horses and sheep, graze on grass and other ground plants. Other herbivores, such as deer and giraffes, feed on leaves, shoots, and fruits from bushes and trees.

First stop

Swallowed food goes into the large stomach chamber, the rumen.

Feeding twice

Herbivores such as cows, camels, and giraffes are ruminants. They chew and swallow food that passes into one part of the stomach, the rumen, for partial digestion. Then they bring it up and chew it again, called "chewing the cud," before swallowing it a second time for further digestion.

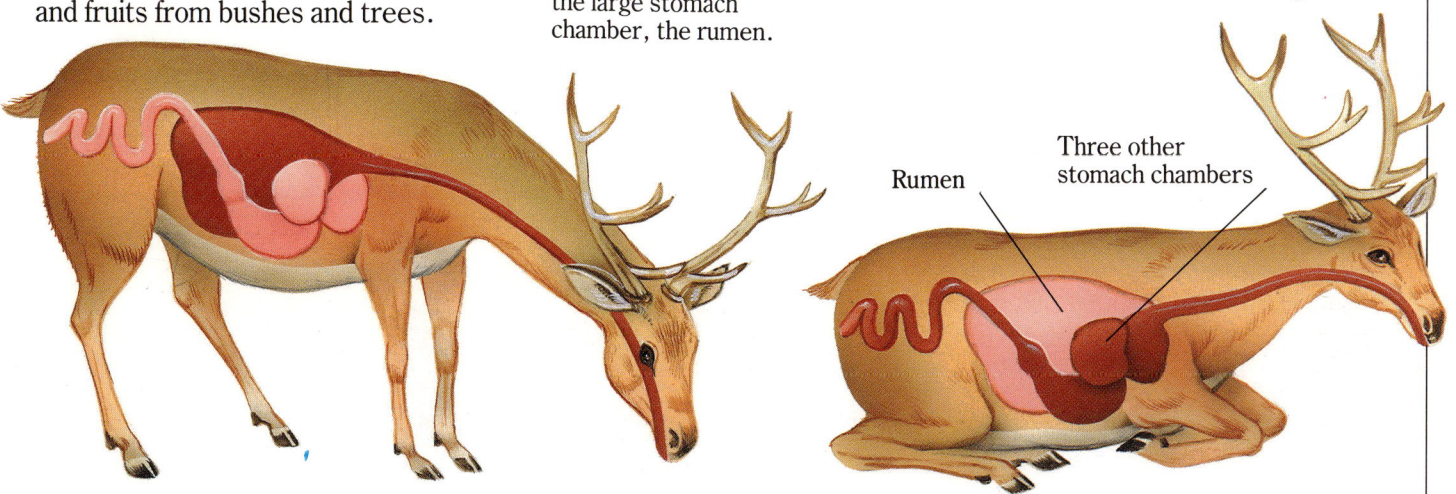

Rumen

Three other stomach chambers

What Animals See?

VIEWS OF THE WORLD

We can guess at what an animal's eye detects by the structure of the eye. But we cannot really know what the creature "sees" in its brain, in its "mind's eye."

An insect as a human would see it.

The same view seen by another insect.

An insect seen by the powerful eyes of a hawk.

We know that animals can see certain objects, colors, and movements, by observing them in the wild and testing them in zoos and laboratories. For example, in nature at breeding time, certain animals try to impress their mates by displaying beautifully colored skin, feathers, scales, or fur. So we assume that the animals can see those colors, or there would be no point in having them.

Tests show that many animals cannot see colors as well as humans can. For example, food may be placed behind one of several doors. An animal may not be able to pick out a door of a certain color, but it may be able to pick out a door by its size or by the pattern on it.

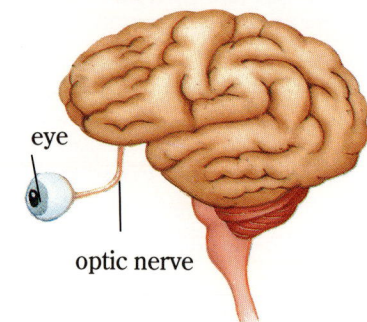

Eye, nerve, and brain
Each eye is connected to the brain by a nerve known as the optic nerve. Nerve signals pass along the optic nerve to the brain's visual center (see page 8).

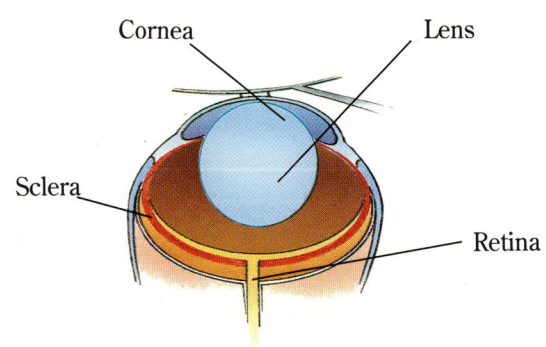

Fish
A fish has a rounded eye with a large, bulging lens, for seeing clearly underwater.

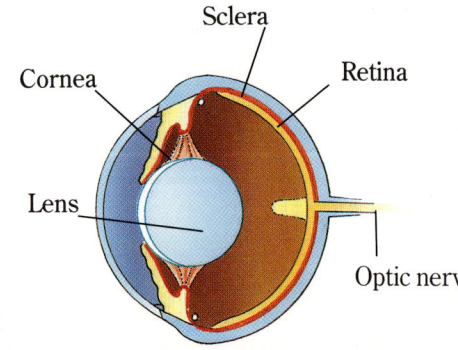

Snake
Snakes have no eyelids, which gives them their "glassy stare" appearance.

Different eyes
Vertebrates (see page 4) all have the same basic design of eye. The sclera is the eyeball's tough outer lining. The cornea is the clear front part that lets light in. The lens focuses the light rays for a clear, sharp view. The retina detects light rays and changes them to nerve signals.

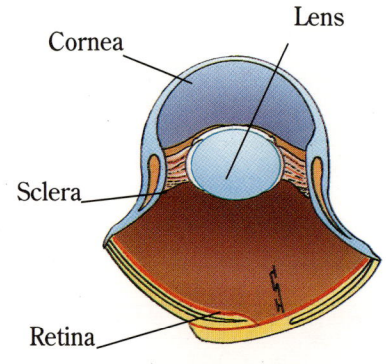

Eagle
The back of the eye is very wide, to give an amazingly detailed view, even at a great distance.

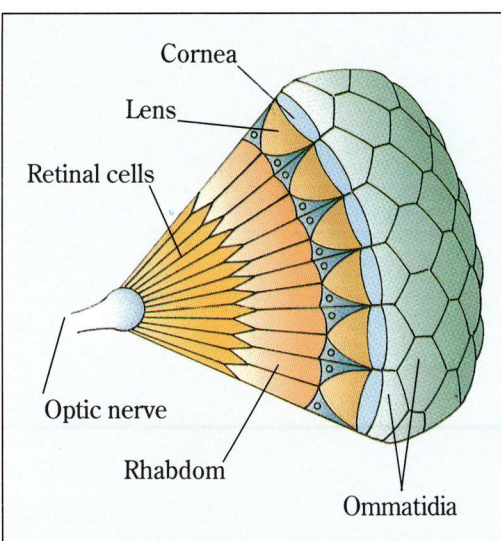

INSIDE THE FLY'S EYE
An insect's eye is made of many rod-shaped units called ommatidia. Each one has its own cornea, lens, and light-sensitive rod, the rhabdom. This changes light into nerve signals for the retinal cells. Each ommatidium detects a small part of the view. These many small sections of the scene may be combined in the insect's brain to give a mosaic-type view of the world.

Cornea
Lens
Retinal cells
Optic nerve
Rhabdom
Ommatidia

Eyes on stalks
A snail has simple "eyes" at the ends of stalks, or tentacles. They cannot see a detailed view. They detect patches of light and darkness and moving shadows, warning the snail that something is coming near.

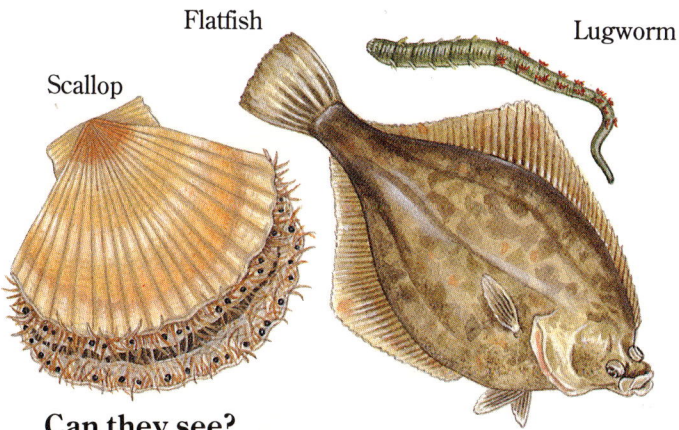

Flatfish
Lugworm
Scallop

Can they see?
Many creatures have simple light-detecting organs, which sense light and dark areas. The jewellike eyes around the rim of a clam or scallop respond quickly to sudden darkening, which is normally caused by a predator swimming above. The earthworm has single-celled eyes scattered over its skin, which warn when light is too bright (see page 14). The flatfish has two eyes on the same side of its head!

How much can they see?
The size and position of eyes give clues to what an animal sees and its life-style. Big eyes gather lots of light for seeing in dim conditions. Eyes on the side of the head are good at keeping an all-around watch for predators. Tiny eyes or none at all means an animal lives in very dark conditions, such as underground, in a cave, or deep in the ocean.

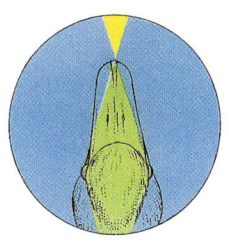

Duck
Eyes on the side of the head see to the sides, and even behind. But there is a blind area at the front, around the beak.

Monkey
Eyes that face mainly to the front see two overlapping views of the same scene. This helps to judge distances accurately.

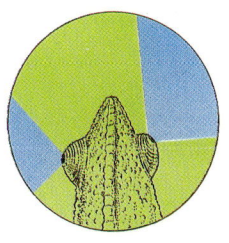

Chameleon
This lizard has two eyes on moving turrets, which can point in different directions. It sees two separate views.

What Animals Hear?

We can test how animals respond to certain sounds, both in the wild and in captivity. We watch their reactions to natural sounds and also to noises recorded on tape. In this way we can find out what sounds are important in an animal's life. A mouse, for example, may "freeze" and stay completely still if it hears an owl's hoot.

As humans, we have difficulty appreciating what animals hear. We mainly rely on our sense of sight; hearing is our "second" sense. However, some animals use hearing as their first sense. It is difficult for us to imagine a world dominated by sounds instead of sights. Also, our hearing has limits. Many animals can hear sounds that are pitched too high or too low for our own ears to detect.

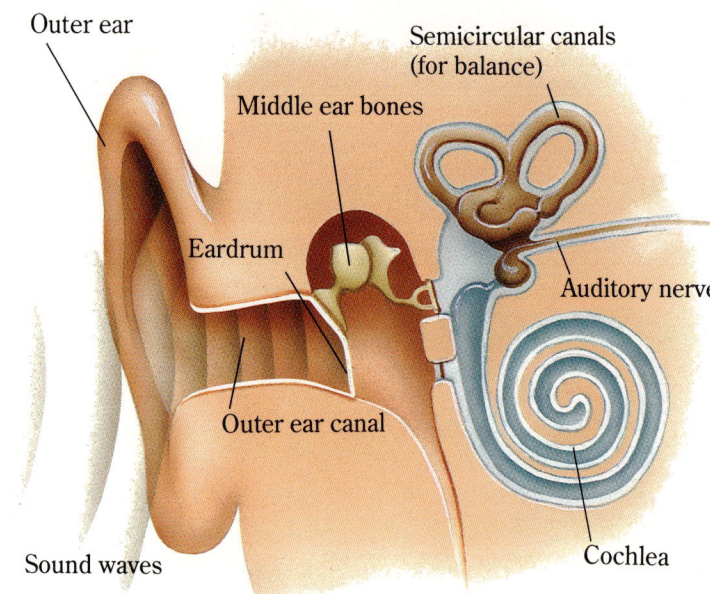

Outer ear

Semicircular canals (for balance)

Middle ear bones

Eardrum

Auditory nerve

Outer ear canal

Cochlea

Sound waves

Inside the human ear
Sound waves hit the eardrum and vibrate a chain of three tiny bones, the ear ossicles. These pass on the vibrations to fluid in the snail-shaped cochlea. The cochlea turns the vibrations into nerve signals and sends them to the brain.

UNDERWATER "EARS"

Most fish have a thin line along each side of the body, called the lateral line. It works like an ear, detecting vibrations and turning them into nerve signals. The fish can "hear" vibrations and currents in the water, and so sense sounds and things moving nearby.

Lateral line

The fennec fox uses its ears to hear and to cool down.

Different ears
We can guess how much an animal relies on its hearing by the size of its ears and by the size of the auditory center in its brain (see page 8). Some animals have large ears that can move and swivel around to detect where a sound is coming from.

Frog's eardrum on side of head

Deer's ears twitch and turn

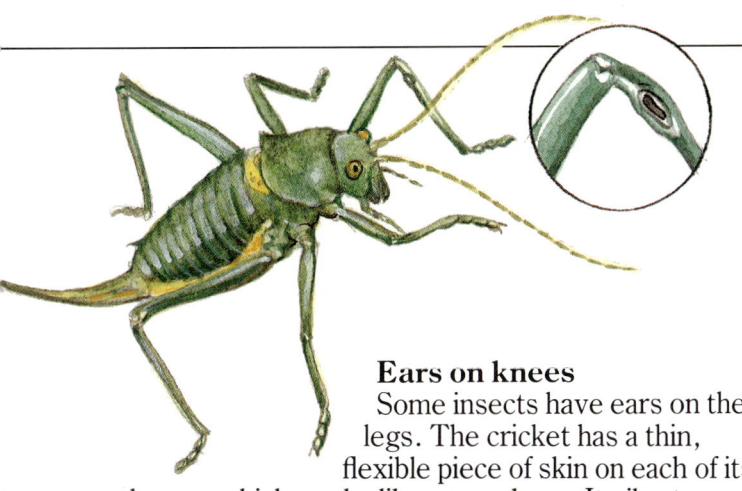

Ears on knees

Some insects have ears on their legs. The cricket has a thin, flexible piece of skin on each of its rear knees, which works like an eardrum. It vibrates when sound waves hit it and sends nerve signals to the insect's brain. Many creatures use sounds to communicate, such as chirping crickets, croaking frogs, and singing birds. Their ears are very sensitive to the sounds made by their own kind.

Very low sounds

Elephants can make and hear infrasounds— sounds that are too deep or low-pitched for our own ears. The very low, rumbling noises travel through the countryside for 1–2 miles (2–3 km). Elephants use the sounds to "talk" to each other.

USEFUL ECHOES

A bat makes high-pitched squeaks and trills of sound, and listens for the returning echoes, in the same way as the dolphin (below). The method of locating the position of objects from the detailed pattern of reflected echoes is termed echolocation.

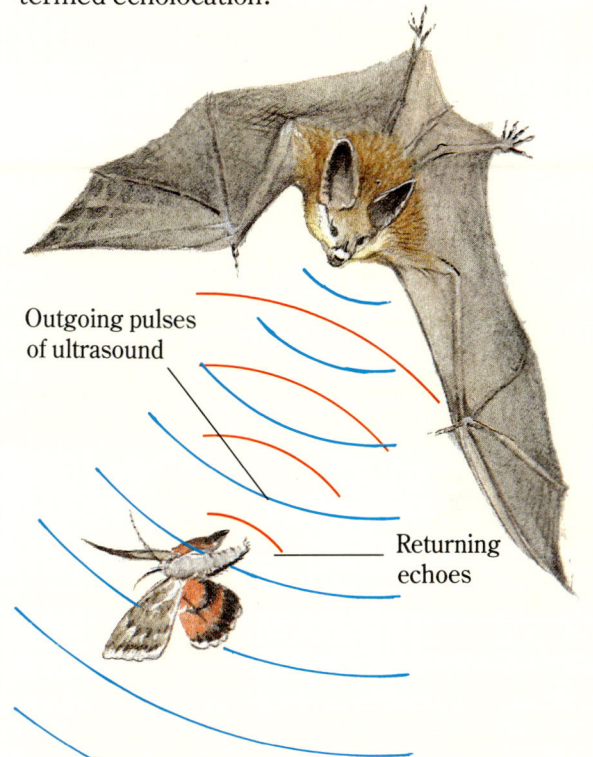

Outgoing pulses of ultrasound

Returning echoes

"Seeing" in the dark

A bat can find its way in pitch darkness, using echolocation. It can detect an object as thin as a human hair from over 3 feet (1 m) away.

Very high sounds

Dolphins can make and hear ultrasounds—sounds that are too shrill or high-pitched for our own ears. Dolphins communicate with each other using many different ultrasonic noises, such as squeaks, whistles, trills, chirps, and clicks. A dolphin can also send out pulses of ultrasound and listen for returning echoes that have bounced off nearby objects. In this way it can locate food, such as a shoal of fish or squid, as well as obstacles like underwater rocks and shipwrecks, and predators such as sharks. Many other animals can hear ultrasounds, too, such as dogs, bats (see above), mice, and moths.

Dolphin makes ultrasonic sounds

Sounds bounce off fish shoal

Sonar and radar

Locating objects using reflected sound waves is called sonar. Dolphins use it, and so do submarines. Radar uses **radio waves** instead of sound waves. Air traffic controllers use radar to find the positions of aircraft.

Dolphin detects pattern of returning echoes

What Animals Smell?

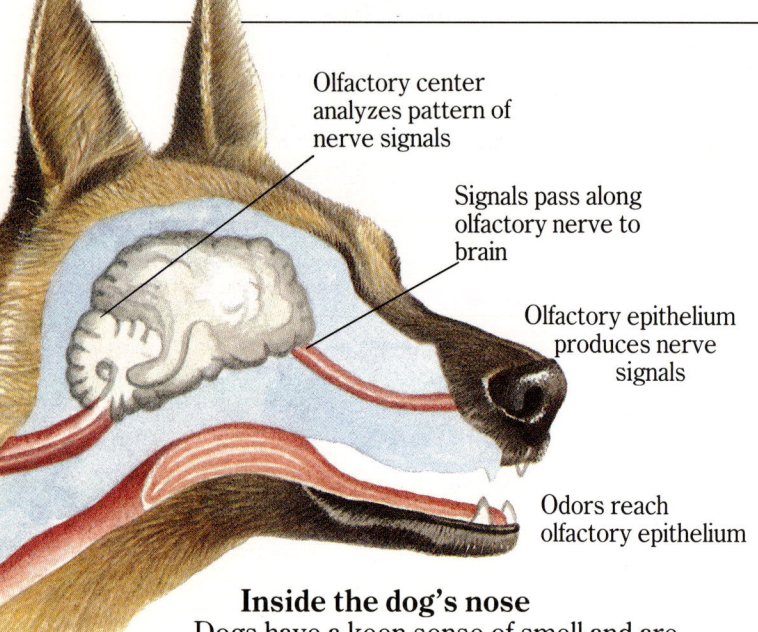

Olfactory center analyzes pattern of nerve signals

Signals pass along olfactory nerve to brain

Olfactory epithelium produces nerve signals

Odors reach olfactory epithelium

Inside the dog's nose
Dogs have a keen sense of smell and are always sniffing around. They smell something before eating it, they smell a place before lying down for a rest, and they smell other dogs to identify them. This shows how important smell is for a dog.

We can find out if an animal responds to certain smells by conducting tests in **captivity** and making observations in the wild. But it is difficult work. We cannot use our two main senses, sight and hearing, to detect smells and odors. Compared to many other animals, our own sense of smell is not especially good. Machines we devise to sense smells are not very sensitive or accurate, compared to such devices as cameras for light and microphones for sounds. So detailed knowledge of the "smell picture" that an animal detects is very difficult to obtain.

This bias toward sight and hearing also means that we have difficulty in understanding how some animals use smell as their main sense. Their world is dominated not by sights or sounds but by scents.

MATING SMELLS

Sometimes an animal finds its way, even in complete darkness and silence. It is probably navigating by smell. Some male moths can fly directly to a female more than 2 miles (3 km) away. This is because the female gives off a special scent called a pheromone, which is detected by the male's feathery antennae (feelers).

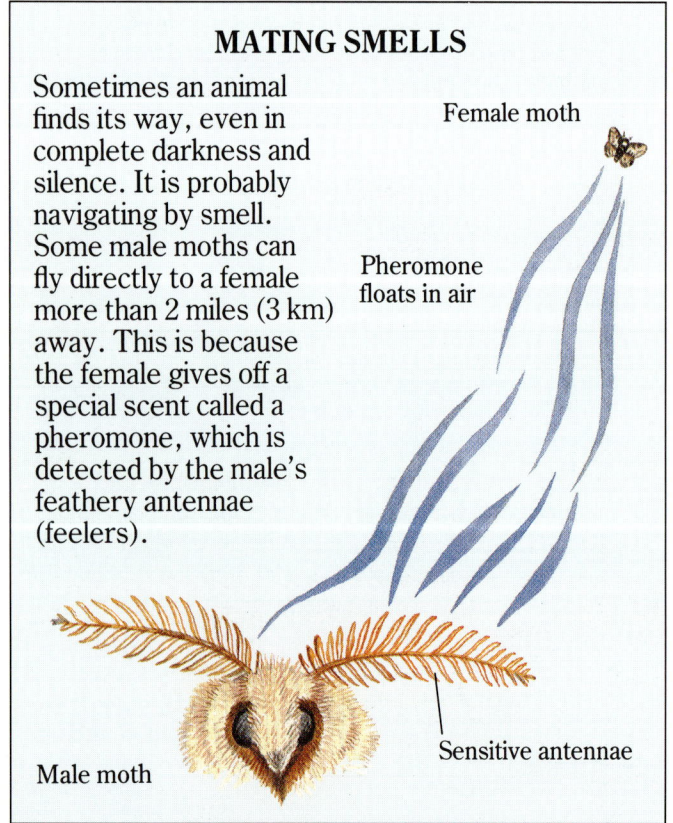

Female moth

Pheromone floats in air

Sensitive antennae

Male moth

Food smells
Most birds have good sight and hearing, and poor smell. But the kiwi has an excellent sense of smell. It sniffs odors through the nostrils at the tip of its beak. By probing into the soil and sniffing, it can locate worms, insects, and other small creatures up to 4 inches (10 cm) below the surface.

Tail spray

A foul fluid sprays out from a gland under the skunk's tail.

Defensive smells

Why do animals avoid the skunk? Probably because they remember meeting this animal previously. They got too close and were sprayed by a fluid that smelled awful. The fluid's powerful odor lasts for days and makes the eyes water. The skunk uses its smell as a defensive weapon.

Territorial smells

Some animals have their own area of land, called their territory, where they live and feed. Other animals of the same kind are chased out. The owner marks the boundaries of its territory by smell. It uses odors in urine, or scents from special body glands, which are rubbed on rocks, tree stumps, and other objects. The smell warns others—this territory is taken!

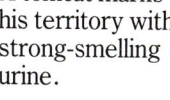

A tomcat marks his territory with strong-smelling urine.

Homing smells

How do adult salmon find their way from the open sea, upriver, to the stream where they were born? The salmon remember the exact chemical makeup, or "smell," of the water. This is very weak when it reaches the ocean, but the salmon can follow the scent trail back to its home stream.

How sensitive is smell?

Smell experiments show that a dog can detect certain odors a thousand times weaker than those detected by a person. The shark's nose is even more sensitive but, like most animals, only to smells that are important in its life. The shark can smell a single drop of blood in a million drops of seawater.

What Animals Taste?

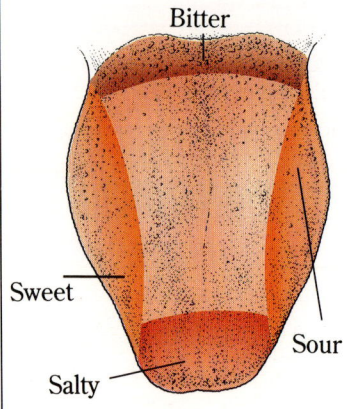

Tasting areas
Different parts of the human tongue detect four basic flavors: salty, sweet, sour, and bitter. All tastes are made from different combinations of these flavors.

It might be a good idea to ask this question another way. What is taste for? You may enjoy the taste of chocolate, or ice cream, or possibly carrots. But you know when something tastes really rotten, or "off," and you know that you should not eat it. It might make you sick, or ill. It might even be poisonous. This is what taste is really for—checking the food that you eat. Most animals know which foods they can eat and which they should avoid by smell and then taste. This is why many animals sniff their food carefully, then lick it a few times. Knowing which tastes are safe is partly built-in or instinctive and is partly gained through experience.

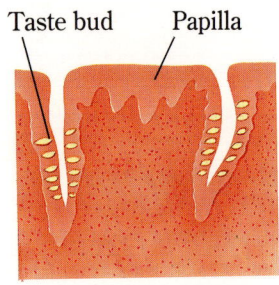

Taste buds
The flavors in foods are sensed by microscopic bunches of cells called taste buds, scattered over and between the larger lumps (papillae) on the tongue.

TASTING FEET?

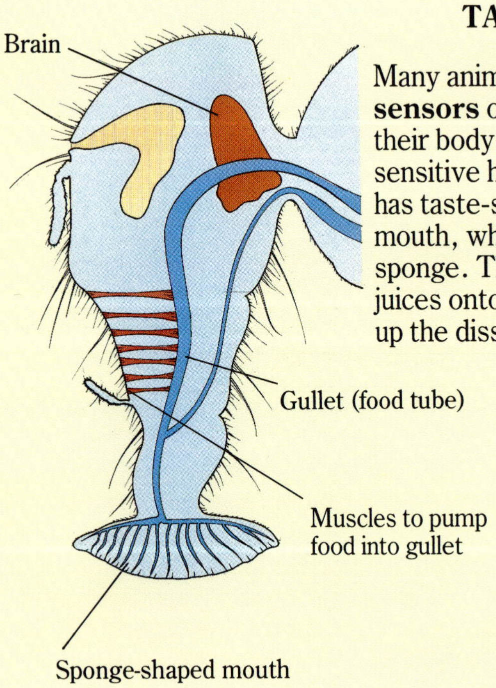

Many animals have taste **sensors** on several parts of their body. The fly has flavor-sensitive hairs on its feet. It also has taste-sensitive parts on its mouth, which is shaped like a sponge. The fly spits digestive juices onto its food and sucks up the dissolved mixture.

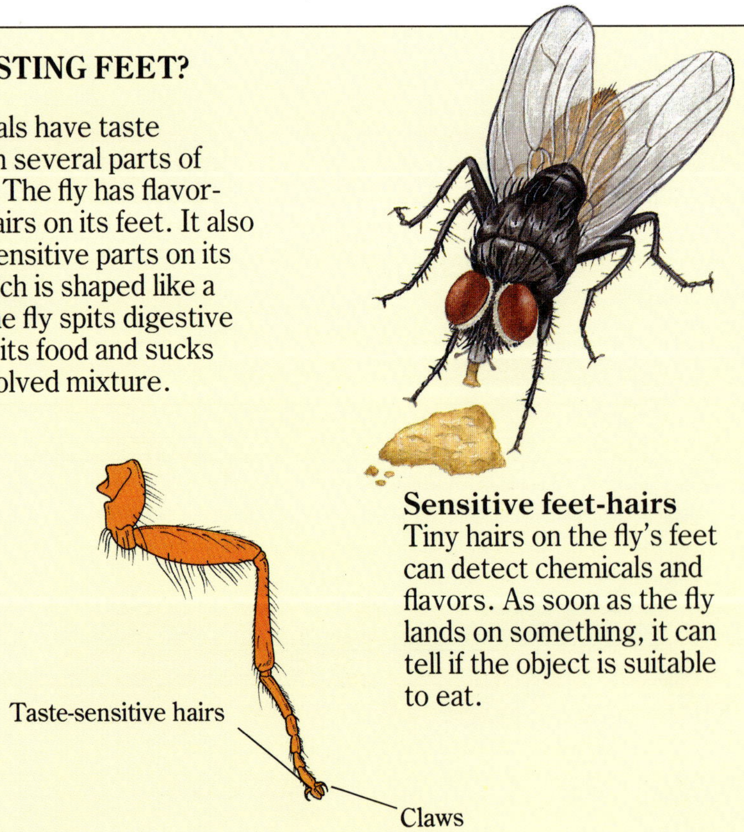

Brain

Gullet (food tube)

Muscles to pump food into gullet

Sponge-shaped mouth

Taste-sensitive hairs

Claws

Sensitive feet-hairs
Tiny hairs on the fly's feet can detect chemicals and flavors. As soon as the fly lands on something, it can tell if the object is suitable to eat.

Tasting all over
On land, there is a difference between smell and taste. Smells float in the air; tastes are in the food. In water, there is little difference between the two, and they are both called chemosenses. A catfish has so many chemosensors scattered all over its skin that it has been called a "living tongue."

Feelers (barbels) have lots of chemosensors.

Tasting arms
Why does an octopus spend so much time feeling its food before putting a piece in its mouth and tasting it? Experiments show that the octopus is "tasting with its arms." The arms have chemosensors on them, and the octopus can identify bad-flavored food simply by touching it. It is as if you could taste through your fingertips!

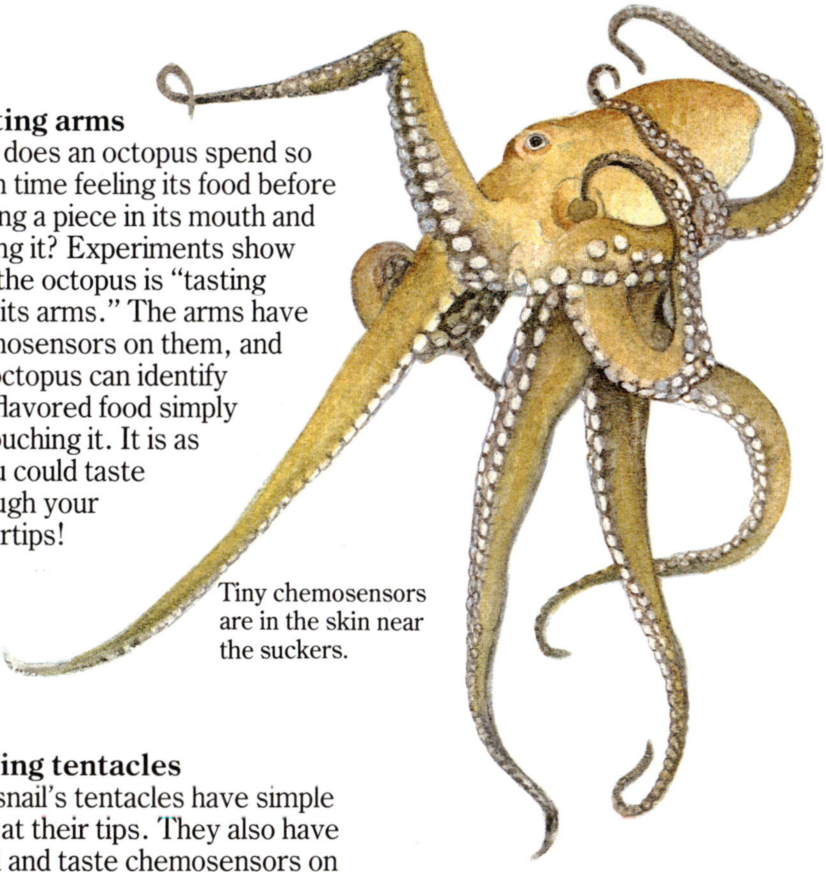

Tiny chemosensors are in the skin near the suckers.

Tasting tentacles
The snail's tentacles have simple eyes at their tips. They also have smell and taste chemosensors on them. These can detect odors floating in the air and flavors when touching food. If in danger, the snail draws its tentacles into its body to prevent them from being damaged.

TASTE AS DEFENSE
In the same way that the skunk uses smell as defense (see page 25), some animals use terrible taste to defend themselves against enemies. The foul flavors are produced by glands in the skin.

Parotid gland

A toad's parotid glands, behind its eyes, produce a horrible-tasting, poisonous fluid.

Taste as a killer
The skin poisons of arrow poison frogs, from Central and South America, are deadly. They can kill an animal that even tries to hold the frog in its mouth.

What Animals Feel?

By this question, we mean "feel" in the sense of feeling touches on the skin. (For other types of feelings or emotions like sadness and joy see pages 32–33). If you pet a tame animal, such as a dog or cat, its behavior shows that it can obviously feel your hand, and it may want to be petted more! You can also feel the touch of the animal's fur on your fingers. If a pesky fly lands on an animal, the animal shakes itself or tries to swish it away.

So would you. In fact, our skin is very similar to the skin of other mammals. We can guess that mammals feel touch in much the same way as we do.

Feeling cold
A cold bird fluffs out its feathers to trap air among them, like an **insulating** quilt. This keeps its body heat in more effectively. A cold mammal does the same by fluffing up its fur.

Pectines

Feeling vibrations
Before you get close to a scorpion, it runs and hides. It has felt your footsteps as tiny shakes or vibrations of the ground. It detects these using feather-shaped parts, called pectines, on the underside of its body.

Feeling different sensations
This is a close-up view of the skin on a typical mammal. Under a microscope millions of miniature touch sensors of several different kinds can be seen. Each kind is sensitive to various features of touch, such as light touch, vibrations, heavy pressure, warmth, cold, or pain.

Feeling hair
A hair is made of dead cells and cannot feel anything. But nerve endings wrapped around the hair's root sense the hair being moved.

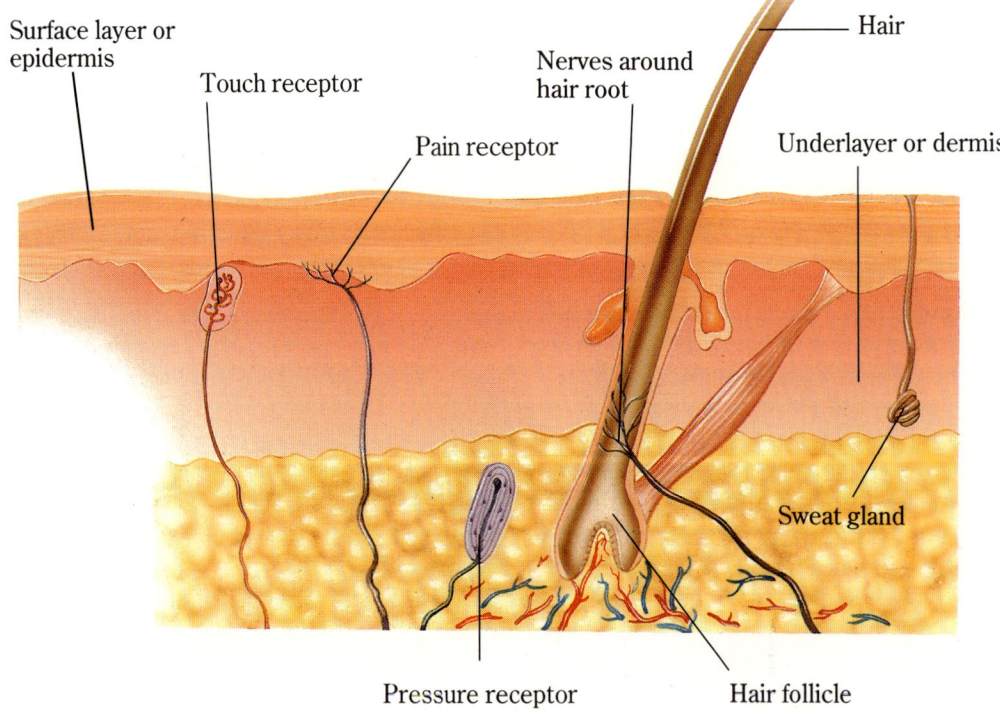

Surface layer or epidermis

Touch receptor

Pain receptor

Nerves around hair root

Hair

Underlayer or dermis

Sweat gland

Pressure receptor

Hair follicle

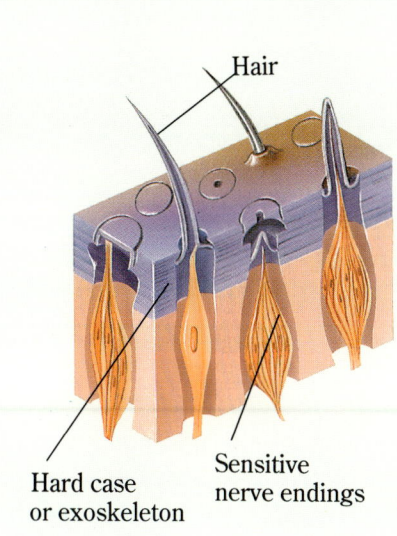

Hair

Hard case
or exoskeleton

Sensitive
nerve endings

FEELING MOVEMENT

An insect has a hard outer casing on its body, called the exoskeleton. This casing is waterproof and gives good protection, but it cannot feel anything. The insect gets its sense of touch from tiny hairs embedded in the exoskeleton. These hairs have nerve endings at their bases, which detect the hair being tilted or rocked. Some of these hairs are also sensitive to chemicals, providing smell and taste (see pages 24–27).

Caterpillar covered in sensory hairs

FEELING IN THE SEA

Like insects (above), crustaceans, such as crabs, lobsters, and shrimp, have a hard outer body shell or casing, which is called an exoskeleton. This has tiny hairs in it, which respond to being touched and waved by water currents.

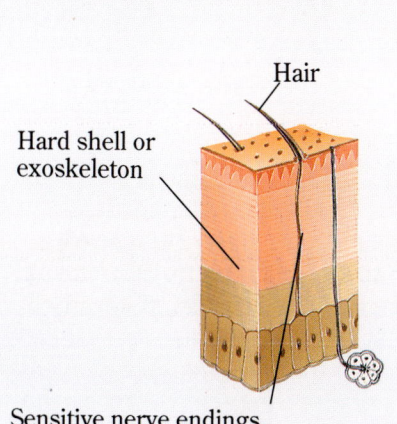

Hard shell or
exoskeleton

Hair

Sensitive nerve endings

Feeling for food

The platypus of Australia has a mouth shaped like a duck's beak, covered by leathery skin. This is very sensitive to touch. The platypus dives into muddy creeks and pools and feels with its beak for food, such as worms, shellfish, and freshwater crayfish.

Whiskers

Whiskers are very long, thick hairs. Like smaller hairs, they have sensitive nerve endings around their bases (see page 28). So the animal can feel the slightest tilt or movement of the whisker. The walrus of cold northern oceans dives into the dark sea and feels in the gloom with its fringe of 500 bristly whiskers for food, such as clams and crabs.

Animals Sense Other Things?

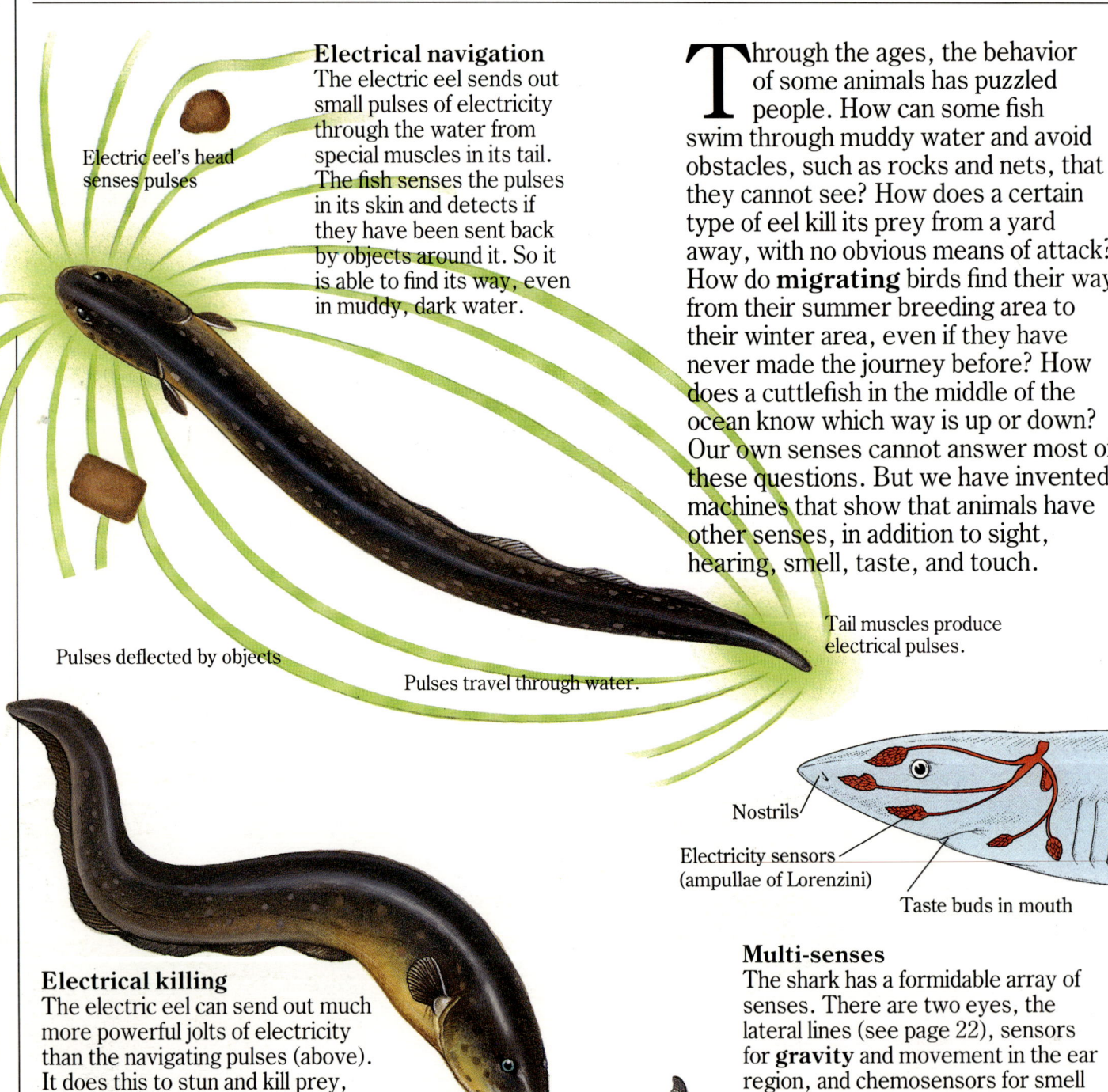

Electrical navigation
The electric eel sends out small pulses of electricity through the water from special muscles in its tail. The fish senses the pulses in its skin and detects if they have been sent back by objects around it. So it is able to find its way, even in muddy, dark water.

Electric eel's head senses pulses

Pulses deflected by objects

Pulses travel through water.

Tail muscles produce electrical pulses.

Through the ages, the behavior of some animals has puzzled people. How can some fish swim through muddy water and avoid obstacles, such as rocks and nets, that they cannot see? How does a certain type of eel kill its prey from a yard away, with no obvious means of attack? How do **migrating** birds find their way from their summer breeding area to their winter area, even if they have never made the journey before? How does a cuttlefish in the middle of the ocean know which way is up or down? Our own senses cannot answer most of these questions. But we have invented machines that show that animals have other senses, in addition to sight, hearing, smell, taste, and touch.

Nostrils

Electricity sensors (ampullae of Lorenzini)

Taste buds in mouth

Electrical killing
The electric eel can send out much more powerful jolts of electricity than the navigating pulses (above). It does this to stun and kill prey, such as small fish and frogs. The electric ray and electric catfish stun prey in this way, too. They use jolts of electricity to deter enemies.

Multi-senses
The shark has a formidable array of senses. There are two eyes, the lateral lines (see page 22), sensors for **gravity** and movement in the ear region, and chemosensors for smell and taste. There are also tiny pits in the skin of the head that detect weak pulses of electricity produced by the swimming muscles of other fish.

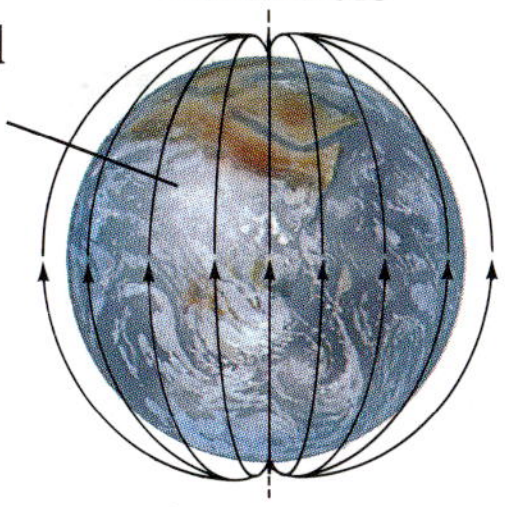

Directional sense

Birds such as terns, swifts, and geese fly thousands of miles during migration. They use a magnetic sense and also a built-in "star map" in the brain to navigate by the positions of the sun, moon, and stars.

North Pole

Lines of natural magnetic force

South Pole

Magnetic sense

How do animals such as birds and whales travel halfway around the world during migration and always arrive at the right place? The mysteries of migration are gradually being solved using special instruments and through experiments. These show that some animals have a magnetic sense, like a built-in "body compass" that can sense the weak natural magnetism of planet Earth.

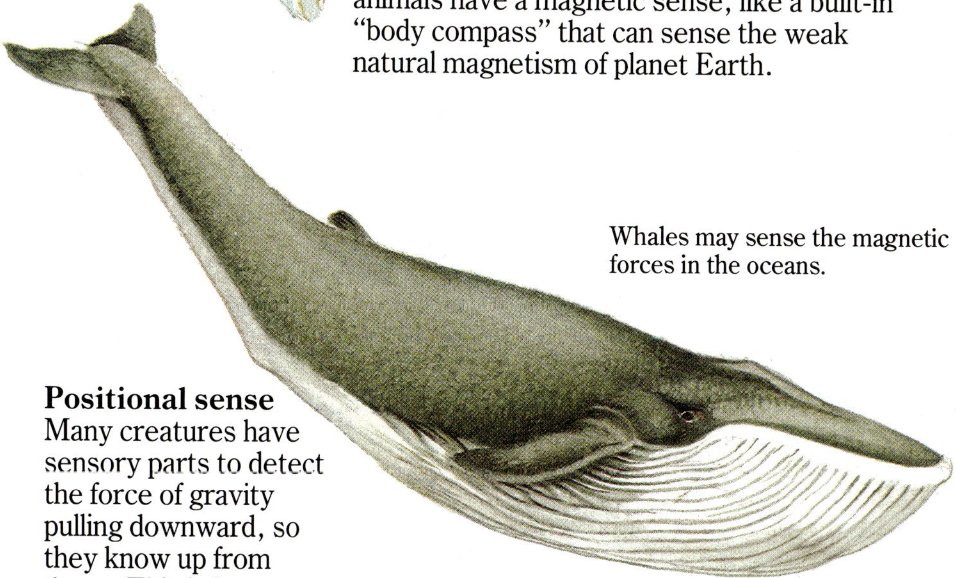

Migrating flies

Whales may sense the magnetic forces in the oceans.

Positional sense

Many creatures have sensory parts to detect the force of gravity pulling downward, so they know up from down. This is important when swimming in mid-water. Octopuses, shrimp, and some worms have sensors called statocysts to detect gravity.

Position of statocysts in a shrimp

FAST-ACTING SENSES

Cats are agile creatures with quick reactions, which depend on fast-working senses. A falling cat uses its senses of sight, gravity, movement, and body position to turn itself upright and get its legs ready to absorb the shock of landing.

What Animals Say?

We have different facial expressions to convey feelings, such as pleasure, fear, and anger. Our close relatives, the apes, also make faces. However, their expressions differ from ours. A chimp who bares its teeth in a "grin" is not pleased but angry.

Animals do not live alone in the world. They encounter other animals in many different situations. As we watch creatures in nature, we can observe that they communicate with each other. Breeding animals communicate with their mates and their babies. Social animals living together communicate with other members of their group. They also communicate with intruders into their home or territory. Animals make contact with enemies and predators.

How? Animals communicate using sights, sounds, smells, tastes, touches, and other methods. We know that a message is detected and understood when the receiving animal reacts with a certain kind of behavior. And we can figure out what an animal is "saying" by the receiver's reactions.

Sounds and songs
Birds sing different songs for different reasons. Their morning song advertises their presence and territorial occupation. Chicks cheep for food from their parents.

Kissing also happens when a member is missing, when an intruder appears, and when a family has become too big, so that a new burrow is needed.

Touching
Prairie dogs of North America live in family groups that dwell close together in a township. Family members spread out to feed but regularly run to each other and "kiss" by touching noses. This helps them to identify and keep in touch with other members of the group.

Sounds and scents

Many animals mark their home ranges or territories with smells to show that the area is occupied (see page 25). Odors and scents have an advantage over sounds. They linger for hours or days, while the animal is elsewhere. The hyena has a bag or pouch under its tail, which it can turn inside out, to smear a smelly, territory-marking paste on plants and rocks. We understand the "message," because if another hyena wanders into the territory and smells the scent marks, it leaves and goes back to its own area. Ants lay invisible scent trails for their nest members to follow to food or water.

Useful droppings

Hippos spread dung in the water and along the riverbank. The smell shows that the stretch of river is taken.

Follow the leader

Worker ants follow an invisible scent trail laid between food and their nest by exploring or scouting ants.

Body language

The position of a dog's mouth, ears, body, legs, and tail show its intentions and "mood." This is called body language. Other dogs understand it and so do people who know about dogs. Wild relatives of dogs, such as wolves and coyotes, have a similar set of body positions and postures.

Aggressive senior coyote

Defensive junior coyote

Long-distance communication

The great whales communicate across vast distances using very loud, low-pitched sounds. Their deep booms and hums may mean several things. The sounds are reflected at "boundaries" formed between layers of water of slightly different temperatures and travel for hundreds of miles through the ocean.

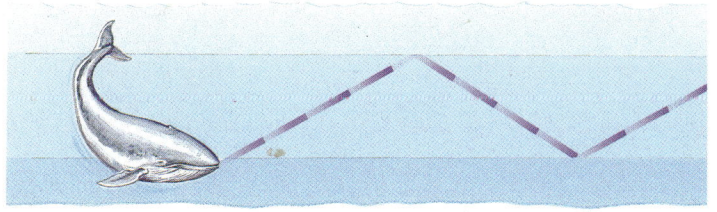

The Breeding Habits of Animals?

COURTSHIP

Male swims a zigzag dance to impress the female.

Female lays her eggs in the nest

Male guards babies in nest

Like many animals, sticklebacks go through a set series of actions, called the courtship ritual.

Studies of wild and captive animals show that many actions and behaviors in their lives are related to breeding. The urge to reproduce is one of the strongest in nature. Some experts believe that the main purpose of an animal's existence is to mate with a partner of its own kind and produce offspring and so continue the species. Some creatures, especially birds and mammals, spend most of their time, energy, and effort in breeding. They build a nest or home, court and mate with a partner, lay eggs or give birth to babies, and defend and care for their young.

Impressing a mate
The male peacock courts a female, or peahen. He fans out his tail and struts around. He shows that he is fit and healthy, and therefore a suitable mate.

Breeding rivals
In some animals that live in groups, males battle with other males for the right to mate with females. Male goats charge each other and butt heads.

TYPES OF BREEDING

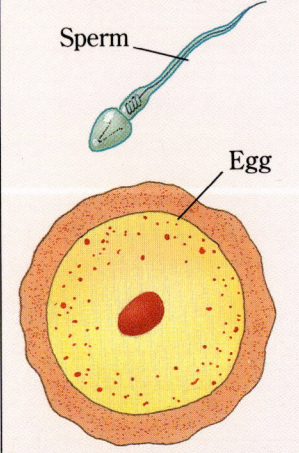

Sperm

Egg

Sexual reproduction
In most animals, a male and female of the same species mate. The female provides the eggs, and the male provides microscopic, tadpole-shaped sperm. When a sperm joins an egg at fertilization, the egg begins to develop into a new animal.

Asexual reproduction
Some animals can reproduce without mating. The hydra is a simple, pond-dwelling animal, a tiny relative of the sea anemone. A new hydra grows on the side of a fully grown hydra and separates to become a new individual. This is called budding.

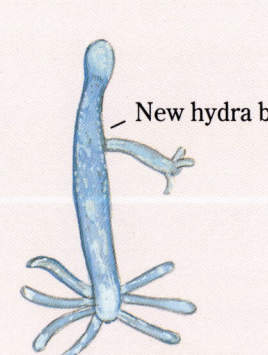

New hydra bud

Parent hydra

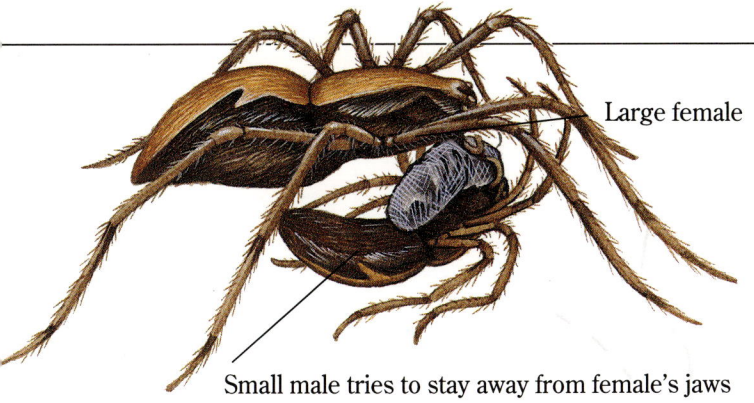

Large female

Small male tries to stay away from female's jaws

Dangers

Breeding can be dangerous for some kinds of spiders and insects, such as mantids. The female is larger and stronger than the male. After mating, the male has finished his "useful life," so the female may eat him!

Parental care

Most birds sit on their eggs to keep them warm and take care of the babies when they hatch. The Australian mallee fowl does not. It lays eggs in a large mound of rotting vegetation, like a compost heap, which keeps the eggs warm. When the young hatch, they must fend for themselves.

Mother aphid

Newborn aphid

Breeding without males?

Breeding experiments show that some female animals can reproduce without having mated with a male. This is a form of asexual reproduction (see page 34) called parthenogenesis. Insects, such as aphids, and some worms do this.

CHANGING SHAPE

Male frog fertilizes spawn

Female frog lays spawn

Fertilized eggs develop.

After three weeks, tadpoles hatch.

After four weeks, external gills disappear.

After seven weeks, back legs develop.

After twelve weeks, front legs appear and tail shrinks

Some animals change body shape during their lives. This change is called metamorphosis, and it occurs particularly in insects and amphibians.

Tadpole has metamorphosed into tiny frog

Animals Rest and Sleep?

We know that animals rest, because we can watch them doing it. A resting animal finds a comfortable place, settles down, relaxes its muscles, and stays still. Its breathing and heartbeat slow down. It may close its eyes. We do exactly the same when we rest, so it is easy to identify the same signs in animals.

Do animals sleep, like people? Scientists have tested the **brain waves** of animals using an EEG (electroencephalograph) machine. The brain waves change, depending on whether the animal is awake and alert, in light sleep, or in deep sleep. The results show that many hunting animals sleep. They have teeth and claws for defense and are unlikely to be attacked. However, many hunted animals sleep very lightly, if at all. They must be ready to sense danger and, in an instant, be alert and ready to escape.

A place to sleep
Animals choose a relatively safe place to rest. This leopard lies on the thick branch of a tree. It is out of the way of most animals and allows the leopard to see and hear anything that comes near.

Active by day
Some animals rest at night and are active by day. Such animals, which include humans, are said to be diurnal. These light-active creatures tend to depend mainly on their sense of sight.

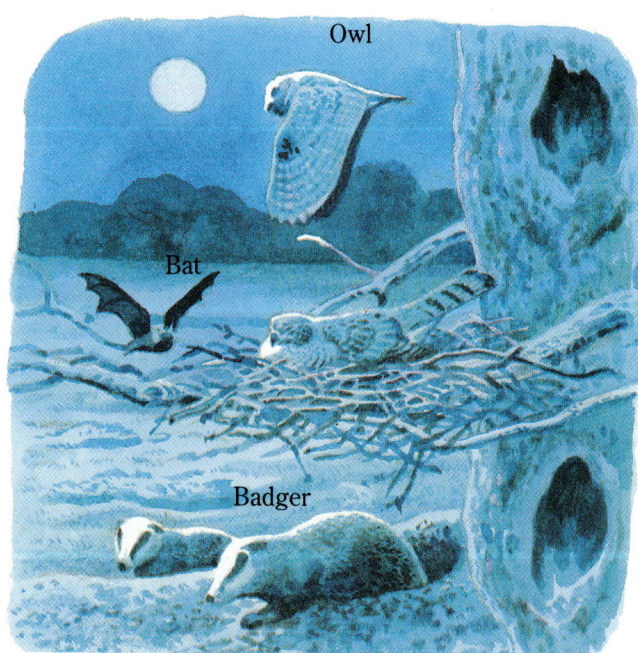

Active by night
Other animals rest by day and are active at night. They are called nocturnal, and many are unfamiliar to us. These dark-active creatures tend to depend on their senses of hearing, smell, and touch.

Horse stands up and closes its eyes, but listens with its ears

Flamingo closes one eye only

Giraffe may sit down but does not lie down

Sleeping positions

Not all animals lie down to rest. Creatures that are hunted may sleep lightly, standing up so that they can run off. Their senses are alert for signs of danger.

THE DEEPEST SLEEP

Some animals go into a very deep sleep called hibernation. They do this to survive the bad conditions of winter, when food is scarce. A sleeping animal uses little energy, so it needs little food. The body cools down, and the heartbeat and breathing are very slow. The animal lives on stores of body fat until it wakes in spring.

Hibernating dormouse

Fairly deep sleep

Other creatures sleep deeply for several days at a time in winter to save energy. But their bodies do not slow down and become cool like a true hibernator. They can wake up and become active on mild days.

Sleepy squirrel wakes up to feed on mild winter days

Forced to rest

The activity of cold-blooded animals, such as fish, frogs, lizards, and snakes, depends on the temperature of the surroundings. If it is warm, then the animal is warm, and it can move around. If it gets too cold, the animal's body cools down. It is not resting— it is too cold to move.

Dawn—The lizard is too cool from the night before to move fast.

Mid-morning—The lizard is warm and moves rapidly.

Midday—The lizard is too hot and cools off in the shade.

What Animals Think About?

It is not possible to get inside the "mind" of an animal, to know exactly how it thinks, and what it thinks about. As humans, we have complicated and sophisticated thoughts, using words, images, and picture symbols. It is doubtful if an animal thinks in such a complicated, language-based way. However, an animal may have its own simple "mind language," which is connected to the basic, important things in its life. These include getting food and water, finding or making shelter, resting, courting and breeding, and avoiding predators and unfavorable conditions. If we watch animals in their natural surroundings, we can see how these important features make them think and behave as they do.

Otter
Feeding takes up a large part of a creature's life. Much of what it thinks about is directed at obtaining food, or at avoiding becoming food. The otter creeps cautiously along the riverbank. It listens and watches for ripples in the water that reveal its fishy food. It also sniffs and listens for signs of danger.

Mayfly nymph
The mayfly nymph is the larva, or young stage, of the mayfly. It lives underwater, eating water plants and bits of debris on the bottom. If a shadow passes above, the nymph runs under a stone for shelter.

Fish
Many fish grub around on the river bottom for worms, insects, and other food. The fish may squirt a jet of water from its mouth to wash away mud and reveal its food.

FOOD CHAINS

First links in the chain
The feeding links between animals make up a sequence called a food chain. In this simple example, a caterpillar eats the leaves of a plant. A bird catches the caterpillar and takes it back to its riverside nest to feed to its chicks.

Next links in the chain
A hungry otter approaches, hears the chicks cheeping, pulls down the nest, and eats them. This is the fourth link in the food chain: leaf > caterpillar > bird > otter.

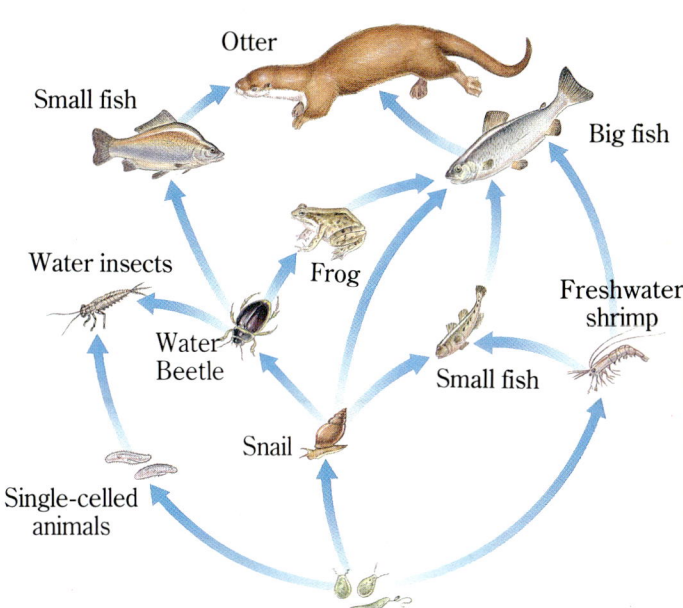

Microscopic animals and plants in the water

Food webs
Nature rarely has single, simple food chains. Each animal eats a variety of foods. So chains link together into a food web. In the two food chains on the left, the otter is at the end. Few animals prey on otters. The feeding habits of animals along a river and riverbank come together as a food web, with the otter at the top.

Do animals have fun?
Some animals show certain behaviors that seem to have no important use. It does not appear to be connected with feeding, breeding, or avoiding danger. Otters slip down mudslides, jump around, and seem to "play." Perhaps humans are not the only ones who can think of having fun!

Glossary

Amphibians
A class of animals that live part of their life in water and part of their life on land

Blood supply
The blood that passes through a body part, bringing oxygen, nutrients, and other essential substances. It flows through tubes called blood vessels.

Brain waves
Tiny electrical signals that pass along nerve cells in the brain. These can be detected by delicate electrical equipment.

Captivity
When an animal is kept in a certain place, such as a zoo, aquarium, aviary, or wildlife park, and not allowed to roam free

Cell
The "building block" of life; the basic tiny part or unit of a living thing

Chemicals
The basic ingredients making up all substances and objects

Digest
To break foods into smaller, simpler bits, ready to take into the body

Energy
The ability to do work and make things happen. Energy comes in many forms, such as light, heat, electricity, chemicals, and movement.

Filter
To separate out particles or objects of a certain size, from whatever they are in. A sieve or net works as a filter to scoop things out of water.

Gills
Feathery-looking body parts of water animals such as crabs, fish, and tadpoles. They are for "underwater breathing." Gills have a good blood supply and take in oxygen dissolved in the water.

Gravity
The force that pulls us, animals, and all other objects down to the Earth. Gravity makes things fall downward and keeps them on the ground.

Insulating
Preventing heat or electricity from passing through. A thick blanket or layer of fur is a good thermal (heat) insulator. Plastic is a good electrical insulator.

Larva
The immature, developing stage of an animal, which grows and changes shape to become the adult. A tadpole is the larva of a frog. A caterpillar is the larva of a butterfly or moth.

Mammal
A warm-blooded vertebrate animal

Migrating
Moving at the same time and to the same place each year

Nectar
Sugary, sweet, syrupy liquid produced by flowers to attract creatures such as insects, birds, and bats. The creatures feed on it and also carry pollen grains from one plant to another, thereby helping the flowers to breed.

Nervous system
The brain and nerves of an animal that enable the animal to detect sensations, think, behave, react, and move

Nutrients
Substances in food that the body uses for growth and repair, and to provide energy for life processes

Organs
Part of a plant or animal that has a certain function, shape, or structure, such as the brain, heart, intestines, bones, and muscles

Oxygen
A gas that makes up one-fifth of normal air. It is an essential ingredient in the chemical processes that get energy from food, to power the processes and activities of living things.

Peripheral
In or on the outside, or around the outer edge. In an animal, the peripheral nerves are those in the "outer" parts of the body, such as the arms and legs.

Radio waves
Invisible waves that travel through air or space at the speed of light and are detected by a radio receiver. They are partly electrical and partly magnetic in nature, similar to light rays.

Reptiles
Animals with dry scaly skin, a backbone, and a bony skeleton

Sensors
Human-made devices or parts of living things that sense or detect something. A camera or an eye senses light, and a microphone or an ear senses sound.

Sonar
Using sound waves to detect the position and size of an object, usually underwater. Sonar is like radar but with sound waves instead of radio waves.

Index

© Simon & Schuster
Young Books 1994